The Used Car Buyer's Manual II

HOW TO GET THE BEST BUY ON A PRIVATE-PARTY SALE

DAVID J. BUECHEL

PYRAMID WEST PUBLISHING

Disclaimer

The purpose of this book is to educate and entertain. It is designed to provide information in regard to the subject matter covered. Every effort has been made to make this manual as complete and as accurate as possible. However, in the purchasing of a used car, there are problems, both observable and unobservable, that are too numerous to cover in a book. Therefore, the buyer assumes all risks and should always beware when purchasing a car. The author and Pyramid West Publishing shall have neither liability nor responsibility to any person or entity with respect to any loss or damage caused, or alleged to be caused, directly or indirectly by the information contained in this book. This manual should only be used as a general guide and not as the ultimate source for car buying.

The Used Car Buyer's Manual II
Copyright © 1996 by David J. Buechel

All rights reserved. No part of this book may be reproduced in any form or by any mechanical or electronic means including information storage or retrieval systems without permission in writing from the publisher, except by a reviewer, who may quote brief passages in a review. Printed in the United States of America. For information address Pyramid West Publishing, P.O. Box 830, Newbury Park, CA 91320.

Illustrations by Edward J. Buechel

First Edition

Library of Congress Catalog Card Number: 96-92359

ISBN 0-9647780-1-7

Acknowledgments

First of all I would like to thank my Mother and my Father for teaching me some smarts. Thanks, Dad, for the expert illustrations, too. Not bad for an ex-sign painter. I would also like to thank Linda Jordan for her patience, understanding, and moral support and all the free photocopying; proofers Lori Lord, Allyson Martin, and Terri Nigro, who bailed me out of punctuation hell; and John Thomson who also made a contribution to this book.

TABLE OF CONTENTS

Introduction

PART I:
HOW TO BUY A USED CAR FROM A PRIVATE PARTY

Chapter 1: Research   13
    1. The Good, the Bad, and the Ugly   13
    2. Used Car Classifications   14
    3. Options to Consider   15
    4. Best Used Car Bets   16
    5. The Library   18
    6. The Blue Book   19
    7. Recall Information   20
    8. Resale Value   20
    9. The Phone Book   21
    10. Word of Mouth   22
    11. Selecting a Mechanic   23
    12. Scan the Ads   23
    13. Financing   26
    14. Auto Insurance   28

Chapter 2: The Search   29
    15. Are You Ready?   29
    16. Interpreting an Ad   30
    17. Questions to Ask   30
    18. Get an Appointment   35
    19. Excuses, Excuses   36
    20. Cars with Out-of-State Plates   37
    21. City Miles Vs. Freeway Miles   38
    22. Don't be Hasty   38
    23. Dangling Carrots   39

Chapter 3: Checking Out the Beast   41
    24. Some Firsthand Tips   41
    25. A Word About Color   42
    26. How to Check for Body Damage from an Accident   43
    27. How to Check for Body Damage from Rust   46
    28. Tires and Suspension   48
    29. Fluids to Check   49
    30. Check Air Filter, Belts, and Hoses   50

31. Things to Leak Out For   51
  32. California Emissions   53
  33. The Tail Pipe   54
  34. Check the Glass   54
  35. About Sunroofs   54
  36. Interior   55
  37. Luggage Compartment   56
  38. Flood Cars   57

Chapter 4: The Test Drive   59
  39. Listen with Your Ears   59
  40. Check the Brakes   61
  41. About Brake Noises   61
  42. Check the Alignment   62
  43. Check the Transmission   62
  44. The Open Road   63
  45. About Receipts   64
  46. The Character Thing   65
  47. A Waste of Time and Money?   66
  48. Going to Your Mechanic   67
  49. Double Check for Recalls   68

Chapter 5: Negotiating   71
  50. Phase 1: Preconditioning   72
  51. Phase 2: Negotiating Before the Mechanic's Inspection   73
  52. Phase 3: Negotiating After the Mechanic's Inspection   76
  53. Emotion Control   78
  54. Other Negotiation Tips   79
  55. Transfer of Vehicle Ownership   80
  56. Salvage Titles   82

PART II:
HOW TO SELL YOUR USED CAR

Chapter 6: Selling Your Used Car   85
  57. Prepping Your Car for Sale   86
  58. The Lazy Person's Way   87
  69. The Person-with-a-lot-of-Energy Way   87
  60. California Residents Only   88
  61. Asking Price   88
  62. Advertising   89
  63. The Phone Calls   91
  64. The Appointment   92
  65. Negotiating   94
  66. A Few Last Tips   96

PART III:
CARING FOR YOUR USED CAR

Chapter 7: Car Care   101
    67. Your Owner's Manual   101
    68. About Oil   103
    69. Oil Burners   104
    70. Other Fluid Concerns   105
    71. Lube Centers   106
    72. Tires   106
    73. Engine Ping and Gasoline   107
    74. Tune-Up   108
    75. Repair Fraud   109
    76. Engine Warm-Up   109
    77. Car Care Tips   110

Appendix A: Directory of Reliable Used Cars   116
Appendix B: Vehicle Inspection Checklist   118

Introduction

This book is dedicated exclusively to the used car buyer who wants to get the best possible deal on their next purchase through a private-party sale. It does not cover dealer sales. If you think there may be a chance that you will buy through a dealer, the original *Used Car Buyer's Manual* offers everything that this book has with the addition of two complete chapters on dealing with dealers to prepare you for combat. Order information for either guide is in the back of this book.

There are many books written on the subject of car-buying, yet strangely enough, none of them cater to buyers who get their cars from private-party sellers. After reviewing a multitude of car-buying guides, I found that most focused on how to beat the dealer on new or used car deals or both. In a couple of these books, the most information that I could find on private-party sales dedicated only one chapter to the subject.

The strange thing about this is the fact that, on an annual basis, millions of more consumers buy used cars from private sellers than from dealers. More and more people are finding that the best deals to be had are through private-party deals.

The reason for this is the simple fact that private sellers are not dealers, they are just people like you and me on the same level as the rest of us which makes for a relaxed sale. There's no office to sit in hour after hour while some slick-talking salesman wears you down. You buy at your own pace. And with no unfair advantages between buyer and seller, it's not difficult to bargain them down which is where some huge savings can be made. In most cases, a price can be reached within 10 minutes of stress-free negotiations. It's like a dream come true. You will always get the most car with the least amount of money when eliminating the middle-man.

But wait, not so fast you say. What about the fact that I know nothing about the mechanics of cars and, worse yet, I'm buying "as is"? If a major problem should arise and I have no warranty to fall back on, my dream come true could turn into a nightmare.

Don't fret. You need not be Joe Mechanic to know how to look at a car. With all the tips and detailed advice revealed in this book, and your common sense, you will be on the road to a great deal in no time. But you must have some faith in yourself. You really can do it. It's not that hard. With a little effort, anyone can do what I prescribe in this book.

As for the "as is" thing of buying a car without a warranty, having the car checked out by a mechanic will become your safety net. Much more information on this topic is presented in the book.

Within the scope of car-buying, this guide also offers a reliable used car directory in Appendix A which can save you time and legwork by immediately starting you off on the right foot. Everyone knows that not all cars are created equal. Instead of having to spend hours at the library reading up on automotive ratings to weed out the reliables from the undesirables, I have already done that for you. This creates a nice shortcut to making a wise used car investment.

As for the auto inspection, there's no need to take notes because I have already done that for you too. In Appendix B you will find a six page copy-friendly inspection checklist. It follows the steps in the vehicle inspection and test drive chapters almost verbatim, making it as convenient as possible for you to perform a thorough examination.

Completing the book, Chapter 6 shows you how to sell your used car for its maximum value. Anyone who needs to sell their old car can put the information revealed here to good use.

As you can see, I tried my hardest to take the misery and the mystery out of car buying. But I didn't stop there. Chapter 7 goes into detail about car care. It wouldn't make much sense to invest in a good used car if you didn't know how to care for it properly, would it?

I spent a year of my life writing this manual and the previous 16 years at the school of hard knocks learning it. Now the ball is your court. With a little time and effort on your part, you can discover in a week or two what took me many years (and much, much more $$$) to learn. Now, without further adieu, the deals are waiting.

PART I:

HOW TO BUY A USED CAR FROM A PRIVATE PARTY

CHAPTER 1:

RESEARCH

THE GOOD, THE BAD, AND THE UGLY

Why research? Because research will reveal the good, the bad, and the ugly things we need to know about cars BEFORE we buy. You wouldn't want someone else's problems, would you? Start thinking of a used car in terms of an investment. After all, it IS an investment. You need dependable transportation to commute to work so you can make a living, right? A second-hand car that continuously breaks down, drains you of your hard-earned money, and depreciates radically would certainly be a bad investment.

However, a reliable auto that never needs anything beyond normal maintenance will depreciate gradually--making it a good investment. That's what this chapter (and the rest of the book) is all about, separating the good from the bad and the ugly.

The first part can all be done on paper, through research, long before you look at any cars for sale. That's the beauty of buying used. With little difficulty, you can find out which cars offer the best track record.

The second part is finding one of those dependable cars that has been well cared for by its past owner(s) and selling at fair market value. In order to capitalize on this kind of investment, you must do your homework. IT ALL BEGINS WITH RESEARCH!

Before we continue, I must assume that maybe you don't know a thing about cars. If so, just let me clarify. You will see the words *make* and *model* used frequently in the coming pages. Just so there isn't any confusion, *make* refers to the auto maker, like Ford, Chrysler, and Toyota, while *model* refers to the maker's product line, like Mustang, LeBaron, and Corolla, respectively.

Another term I use frequently is "bargaining leverage." What I mean by bargaining leverage is, say you looked at a car that was selling for $5,000 and discovered that the car needs new tires. You would then use the cost of new tires as a reason to lower the price. In other words, if new tires cost $300, then you would naturally expect to get the car for $4,700. You're using the worn tires as bargaining leverage.

USED CAR CLASSIFICATIONS

If you already know the type of car you want, fast forward to the **Best Used Car Bets** section on page 16 and seriously consider the cars from my personal picks list. However, if you are uncertain as to what type of car you want at this point, then you have a few more decisions to make. The following autos have been categorized by size and type to help you place yourself and narrow your focus. DO NOT CONFUSE THIS LIST WITH MY PERSONAL PICKS LIST.

Small Cars
Some examples are: Chevrolet Cavalier, Dodge Colt, Eagle Summit, Ford Escort and Festiva, Geo Metro and Prizm, Honda Civic, Hyundai Excel, Mercury Tracer, Nissan Sentra, Plymouth Sundance, Pontiac Sunbird, Subaru Justy, Toyota Corolla and Tercel, and Volkswagon Fox, Golf, and Jetta.

Mid-Size Cars
Some mid-size cars are Buick Century and Regal, Chevrolet Corsica and Lumina, Chrysler LeBaron, Dodge Dynasty, Ford Taurus and Thunderbird, Honda Accord, Mazda 626, Mercury Cougar and Sable, Mitsubishi Galant, Oldsmobile Cutlass Ciera and Cutlass Supreme, Plymouth Acclaim, Pontiac Grand Prix and Grand Am, Subaru Legacy, Toyota Camry, Volkswagon Passat, and Volvo 240.

Full-Size Cars
Some big American boats are Buick LeSabre, Chevrolet Caprice, Dodge Diplomat, Ford Crown Victoria, Mercury Grand Marquis, Oldsmobile Delta 88, and Pontiac Bonneville.

Luxury Cars
It's hard to find a crank-up window in one of these: BMW 850i, Buick Riviera, Chrysler Fifth Avenue, Nissan Maxima, Mazda 929, Oldsmobile 98, Saab 9000, and all models by Cadillac, Infiniti, Jaguar, Lexus, Lincoln, and Mercedes-Benz.

Sporty Cars
Acura Integra, Chevrolet Camaro and Corvette, Ford Mustang, Geo Storm, Honda Prelude, Mazda Miata and RX-7, Mercury Capri, Nissan 240SX, Plymouth Laser, Pontiac Firebird, Toyota Celica and MR2, and Volkswagon Cabriolet.

Sport-Utility Vehicles
These are the off-road types: Chevrolet Blazer, Ford Explorer, GMC Jimmy, Honda Passport, Isuzu Trooper and Rodeo, Jeep Cherokee and Wrangler, Mazda Navajo, Nissan Pathfinder, Oldsmobile Brevada, and Toyota Land Cruiser and 4Runner.

Vans and Trucks
These are self-classifying. You just need to decide if you want to go mini, mid-size, or full-size. What will you be using it for?

Obviously, this is not a conclusive list of everything out there, but rather a random sampling to use as a convenient way of classifying used cars. Once you do decide on the type of car you want, the next logical step would be to consider which features are for you.

OPTIONS TO CONSIDER

Buying a used car is not like buying a new car, where you can walk onto a lot and pick a car with the options you want. Usually you have to take what you can get. But do decide on what major options you want, like standard transmission or automatic, 2-door or 4-door, air conditioning, etc.

   As far as the minor options, such as power windows, power steering, etc., don't get too hung up on having to buy a used car with these kinds of features. You'll only be making life very difficult for yourself when you start to shop. Just consider those minor options as window dressings. If the car happens to come with them, fine. But if it doesn't, don't let window dressings become a deciding factor in your purchase. If you do, you will be looking for a used car with just the "right" features for a long, long time.

The following is a list of options lumped together in three main categories to help you narrow your focus even further.

Passenger cars
For most passenger cars here are some things to consider: sedan, coupe, cabriolet, station wagon, hatchback, mini-van, 8-cylinder, 6-cylinder, 4-cylinder, diesel, 2-door, 4-door, automatic, standard; 4-speed or 5-speed.

Sports cars
For sports cars: coupe, convertible, hatch back, 8-cylinder, 6-cylinder, 4-cylinder, automatic, standard; 4-speed, or 5-speed.

Trucks
And for trucks: flat bed, long bed, short bed, van, utility, 1 ton, 3/4 ton, 1/2 ton, mini, mid-size, full-size, 4-wheel drive, 2-wheel drive, 8-cylinder, 6-cylinder, 4-cylinder, diesel, 2-door, 4-door, standard cab, extended cab, automatic, standard; 4-speed or 5-speed.

This should help you decide on some of the basic features that you'll be faced with. It's your choice. Once you narrow it down, for example, to a 4-door passenger sedan with a 6-cylinder engine and automatic transmission, then you are ready to head for the library.

BEST USED CAR BETS

Whether or not you already know the type of car you want, I strongly recommend something from my personal picks list. Through my own exhaustive research, I have personally selected the following to be the most reliable used cars on today's market. I took into consideration the three R's--reliability, resale value, and recall history. Please remember, how well a car has been cared for is what really decides how long it will last. Any car can end up a lemon if it was neglected for years. But leading you to cars with proven reliability will start you off on the right foot.

Small Cars
Chevrolet Cavalier 1984-'94, Chevrolet Nova 1985-'88, Dodge Colt 1980-'94, Geo Prizm 1989-'94 (previously Nova), Honda Civic 1980-'94, Mazda 323 1986-'94, Nissan Sentra 1982-'94, Plymouth Colt 1980-'94, Subaru Justy 1987-'94, Toyota Corolla 1980-'94, and Toyota Tercel 1984-'94.

Mid-Size Cars
Buick Century 1986-'94, Dodge Spirit 1989-'94 (except turbocharged), Ford Taurus (V6) 1988-'94, Honda Accord 1980-'94, Mazda Protege 1990-'94, Mazda 626 1980-'94, Mercury Sable 1988-'94, Oldsmobile Cutlass 1980-'94, Plymouth Acclaim 1989-'94, Saturn SL, SC, & SW 1991-'94, and Toyota Camry 1983-'94.

Full-Size Cars
Buick LeSabre (3.8 liter) 1985-'94, Chevrolet Caprice 1985-'94, Ford Crown Victoria 1982-'94, Mercury Grand Marquis 1983-'94, Oldsmobile Eighty-Eight 1980-'94, and Pontiac Bonneville 1980-'94.

Luxury Cars
Acura Legend 1986-'94, Lincoln Mark VII 1984-'92, Lincoln Town Car 1981-'94, Nissan Maxima 1981-'94, Toyota Cressida 1980-'92, and Volvo 240 1987-'93.

Zippy Cars
Acura Integra 1986-'94, Honda Prelude 1980-'94, Mazda Miata 1990-'94, Nissan 200/240 SX 1983-'94, and Toyota Celica 1980-'94.

Trucks/Passenger Vans/Sport Utility
Dodge Ram 50 1983-'93, Mazda Trucks 1980-'94, Nissan Trucks 1980-'94, Toyota Trucks 1980-'94, Dodge Caravan 1984-'94, Plymouth Voyager 1984-'94, Mazda MVP 1989-'94, Toyota Previa 1991-'94, Nissan Pathfinder V6 1987-'94, and Toyota 4Runner 1984-'94.

There you have it: the best of the best. Sure, there are plenty of other reliable used cars on the market, and if you choose to look for something not on my list, you won't hurt my feelings. However, for a list of additional reliable used cars, see Appendix A: **Directory of Reliable Used Cars.**

THE LIBRARY

Whether you choose some models from my list or not, I still recommend a trip to the library to find out about a car's background, like the options that were offered for a particular model, recall history, etc. The best place to start reading up on passenger cars and trucks would be in the past April issues of *Consumer Reports* magazine. Each April issue offers their annual automotive report.

Consumer Guide's annual *Used Car Book* which rates cars up to ten years old, is also a highly reputable and recommended source for used car information. *Consumer Guide* also produces two other publications that are worth a look: *Car Comparisons* and *50 Best New Cars*. Both are published once a year. Another source of information is *Kiplinger's Personal Finance Magazine,* which used to be *Changing Times*. Each December issue offers new car information for the upcoming year.

Armed with the above sources, you can research a car's list price when new, its approximate current value, its reliability rating, how it performed in rigorous test drives, any frequent mechanical problems or recalls, rated fuel economy, options that were offered, its body style (from photos), and when it was redesigned.

So, when you have a couple of hours to kill, go down to your local library with plenty of loose change for photocopies and start digging. If you have narrowed the type of car you are researching down to a few models, you can save time and look them up quickly. However, if you're starting from ground zero, it may take a little longer to leaf through and read up on the many different models. If your library is not the kind that stocks back issues of periodicals on the shelf, you'll have to request the issues you want from the reference desk.

Once you focus on several autos from the model years in your price range, make photocopies of all relevent information. You'll want to keep these for later reference. One bit of advice--it is to your advantage not to get hung up on one specific make and model. Leave yourself open to two or three different models that are similar.

For example, if you really like the look of the Ford Taurus, consider the Mercury Sable. If you like Japanese and want a Toyota Camry, consider a Honda Accord or a Mazda 626 as well. You will benefit more when you start to shop because there will be more cars to choose from. More choices translates to more competition, which means a better deal is likely for you.

THE BLUE BOOK

While you're still at the library, check out what the dealer's Blue Book price is on the auto(s) you seek. Most libraries stock a Blue Book or similar price guide, so it would be wise to check yours and make some photocopies while you're there. If your library doesn't have a current Blue Book, you can always call a bank to get a quote. The bank will consider you a potential customer for an auto loan and will be very accommodating.

Edmunds Used Car Prices, which is published quarterly and goes back ten years, will most likely be at your library, too, but you would be better off picking one up at any book store for a few bucks to have as a convenient price guide as you shop around.

To get the right quote from the Blue Book or *Edmunds*, you will need to know the following:

- year, make, and model
- engine size
- standard or automatic
- 2-door or 4-door
- any special packages that were offered like sports or luxury packages, etc.
- 2-wheel drive or 4-wheel drive (if it was an option)
- and mileage

In the case of mileage, deductions are made for cars with high mileage, while value is added for those with low miles. Both price guides will quote a wholesale and retail price. The wholesale price is what you can expect to receive from a dealer for a trade-in, while the retail price is what you can expect to pay to a dealership or a private party.

Through my own experience, I find the prices in *Kelly's Blue Book* to be inflated. There is a big difference between what *Kelly's* quotes and what *Edmunds Used Car Prices* quotes for the exact same cars. The difference can be up to a thousand dollars or more depending on the model. *Edmunds* seems to be a little more realistic in their pricing.

So when you go to buy a car and see that it's selling for five hundred below book, don't think you just found a deal. It may be five hundred above what is quoted in *Edmunds*. *Kelly's Blue Book* is great if you're selling a car, but not when you're buying. So my advice here is to exercise common sense. Use *Edmunds* price guide to your advantage when buying a used car and use *Kelly's Blue Book* to your advantage when selling or trading in.

Although you won't be using the inflated prices from the Blue Book to your advantage when you buy, you'll likely hear sellers quoting from it. That's the perfect time to pull out your *Edmunds* price guide and challenge them.

Keep in mind, don't let the Blue Book or *Edmunds* fool you. They are only price guides and won't fluctuate with the laws of supply and demand. If there are more buyers than product, guess what? That's right, the price goes up. Reverse the scenario--more product and less buyers--and the price goes down.

RECALL INFORMATION

The National Highway Traffic Safety Administration, under the U.S. Department of Transportation, offers a hotline number you can call for up-to-date information on recalls for any model car or truck. The number is 800-424-9393 (for the hearing impaired, the TTY number is 800-424-9153). They need to know the year, make, and model and, at your request, will send you a printout on the car via fax or mail.

Also, each auto manufacturer offers a computer research service making it easy to check out a specific car's recall history. You need the Vehicle Identification Number, which of course you don't have at this time, but when you do find a car you are considering, it is worth it to double check the recall history with the respective maker. I will remind you of this later on.

RESALE VALUE

Ever notice how some cars hold a better resale value while others seem to plummet? High resale value goes hand-in-hand with reliable cars. The market will tell you which cars are dependable, and when the market talks, you should listen. Don't shy away from used cars that seem pricey. In general, all the best rated cars will be commanding the best prices. It's like Darwin's theory of natural selection--survival of the fittest. And you should be pursuing them as well.

If your budget won't allow the year model you had hoped for, consider getting one that's a year or two older. Remember, when it's your turn to sell, you will still have something highly desirable for the next buyer. However, on models in which the resale value seems bargain priced, watch out! There's usually a good reason for it, and you needn't find out the hard way.

If you have decided on a model(s) from the list of reliable cars that I have previously researched in Appendix A, you may fast forward to the **Selecting a Mechanic** section on page 23. Should you choose not to take my advice on one of those reliable cars I have selected, please read the following two sections.

THE PHONE BOOK

Go to the yellow pages and look up Auto Repair. You need to call some repair shops to get a mechanic's opinion. Don't call a dealership service shop or even a private shop that specializes in the kind of car you're after. They may give you a biased opinion, regardless of the truth. The kind of shop you want to call is one that's been around a few years and works on a variety of domestic and foreign cars. This way you know you're getting the opinion of someone who sees a broad range of vehicles day in and day out.

When you call, ask for a mechanic and give the year, make, and model car you're thinking of buying. Ask if there are any bum years put out by the maker that you should avoid. Also ask if there was a certain engine size or feature that you should avoid in these models. You may hear responses like "the turbo-charged 4-cylinder engines in the '82 through '86 models are junk, but the 6-cylinder with fuel injection offered those same years seem to be holding out."

If you're researching for an import, be it Japanese, German, or whatever, make sure you ask about parts availability. If you live in or around a big city, chances are you'll be okay, but if you live in a small town out in the heartland, you could have problems getting parts. And since most of us don't have a week to wait for a part to come in while our car is down, this is a major consideration.

Finally, ask the mechanic for his personal opinion of these particular models. He may highly recommend them, or he may point you toward a different model altogether. Remember, he is up to his elbows in engine repair all day and sees it all, so listen to what he has to say. To get a well-rounded opinion, call at least three different repair shops.

Be careful of a mechanic who immediately tries to sell you something. Sometimes they buy, repair, and sell cars on the side. When you call to get their opinion and they just happen to have that particular model for sale, chances are they have several different cars as well and your honest mechanic may suddenly turn into Dishonest John's Used Cars. Now, the 4-cylinder turbo-charged engine becomes a spunky engine that's great on gas.

Yet, on the other hand, he could be an honest mechanic who avoids the lemons and concentrates on fixing and selling the less problematic cars. Whatever the case may be, just thank him for the tip and mention that you will keep him in mind. You're not ready to make your move yet. The key to making a good auto investment is completing your research.

WORD OF MOUTH

It may sound silly, but asking around is a good way to get an honest opinion straight from the horse's mouth. People aren't afraid to tell you their likes or dislikes about a car they own or have owned. So, ask for an honest opinion from any family, friends, or neighbors who drive the type of cars you're considering.

And now that you're familiar with the cars you seek, you should be able to spot them around town. So, in your daily travels, look for those cars that are on your list and, when the opportunity arises, whether it's at a gas station or the mall parking lot, just come out and ask the owner about his or her car.

You have your choice of approaches. You could ask "I'm thinking about buying one of those new. Have you had any problems with yours?" Or you could just try the honest approach: "I'm looking into getting one of those used. Have you had any problems with yours?" Make sure you find out the year, engine size, and how long the owner's had it so you can take all that into account. Obviously, the opinion of someone who has owned a car a few years holds more credit than the opinion of someone who's had the same car just a few months. If the person has owned it since new or for a number of years, another good question to ask is, "Would you buy another one?"

The thing about the honest approach is that the owner may have a bucket of problems and could see your interest as an opportunity to sell. Any car, regardless of how well it's rated, can end up being a lemon. He, or the previous owner(s), may not have taken care of the car and it's starting to show its neglect. So be wary of anyone suddenly trying to sell you their "great car." If it's so great, then why are they trying to unload it so quick? NEVER BE IN A HURRY TO BUY A USED CAR!

SELECTING A MECHANIC

If you don't already have a mechanic you like or trust and don't have any recommendations from your friends or family, this is what you do. Go through the yellow pages and look under Auto Repair and find several independent shops who work on the type of cars you have targeted. Call each and tell them you are looking to buy a used car and are wondering what they would charge to check it over and compression test it. They should charge no more than an hour for labor (currently around $50).

Also ask how much notice they need to set an appointment once you locate a car. You'd be better off with a mechanic who says he can take it within a day. Once you find a car you like, you don't want to be waiting more than a day to get it inspected or you could lose the sale to someone else. The way to foolproof this would be to have two or three mechanics to call on. If one is too busy, you can call the next one on your list.

SCAN THE ADS

You need to start scanning the ads for used car prices long before you're ready to buy. This is the most accurate way to see what the market is commanding for the year, make, and model you've been researching. This will also help place yourself when figuring how new a car you can afford.

Keep in mind, I am not talking about used car dealership ads. Forget about those. I'm talking about private party ads by people like you and me who are selling a car on their own. The best place to start looking is in the classifieds in your daily newspaper. Weekly "penny saving" flyers that come in the mail or can be found at the grocery store will also advertise used cars. Have a look around at your local convenience store and grocery store for special auto seller publications. Many are photo ads so you can see a picture of the car that's for sale.

Other places worth checking are public bulletin boards posted around grocery stores, hardware stores, post offices, or wherever there's heavy foot traffic. People will post "For Sale" ads, making this a great way to find a deal.

Before I have you rummaging through the auto ads, let's brush up on the typical classified abbreviations used to save space. I know most of this is just common sense, but I still want to run through it quickly so there are no questions later. Here's how some words may appear:

    air conditioning - AC, air, air cond
    anti-lock brakes - ABS, alb, anti lk brks
    automatic transmission - AT or auto
    cassette stereo - cass str
    chrome - chrm
    convertible - conv
    coupe - cpe
    custom - cust
    eight-cylinder engine - 8cyl, V8
    extended cab - extd cab, extra cab, x-cab, cab +
    four-cylinder engine - 4cyl
    four door - 4dr
    four wheel drive - 4wd, FWD
    fuel injection - FI
    hatchback - HB, hatch
    longbed - LB
    manual transmission - MT, man, manual
    miles per gallon - MPG
    or best offer - OBO
    overdrive - OD
    package - pkg
    paint - pnt
    pickup truck - PU
    power brakes - PB, pwr brks
    power door locks - PL, PDL, pwr dr lks
    power steering - PS, pwr st
    power windows - PW, pwr wds
    sedan - sdn
    shortbed - SB
    six-cylinder engine - 6cyl, V6, straight 6
    standard transmission - ST, std, 4-speed, 5-spd
    station wagon - SW, st wgn, wagon
    sunroof - snrf, sun, or moonroof - mnrf
    tilt steering wheel - tilt
    two door - 2dr
    two wheel drive - 2wd
    wheels - whls
    65,000 miles - 65mi, 65m, 65k

RESEARCH 25

Okay, I think you get the picture, but while we're at it I would like to offer some definitions to common classified terminology to help clear the air.

Asking - Whenever you see the word "asking" preceding the price, i.e. "asking $4,500," it translates to: the seller is hoping to get close to $4,500, but is open to lower offers. "Asking" is a green light to negotiating.

Cabriolet - Just a fancy French word for convertible.

Cherry Condition or Cherry - see Mint.

Clean - It's supposed to mean that the body is dentless and rustless and there is no oil leakage from the engine or transmission. But for some, clean just means they went to the car wash before listing it for sale.

Coupe - a two-door hard-top auto with a trunk.

Custom or Customized - whenever you see this word it means not original. It could be bad or it could be good, depending on the item itself. Most of us wouldn't mind a customized stereo, but a custom sunroof can leak and hurt the value of a car.

Mint Condition or Mint - means that the car looks just like it did when it rolled off the assembly line. Unfortunately, this is rarely the case.

Factory - you may see this from time to time. A "factory sunroof" or "factory rims" means the car came that way from the factory. Factory parts are generally more desirable than custom, thereby making the auto more valuable.

Firm - means the price stated is non-negotiable. However, I have negotiated firm prices many times.

Excellent Condition - almost, but not quite mint.

Good Condition - not excellent.

Okay Condition or Looks Okay - translates to used, abused, bruised, beat-up, and thrashed. Don't even waste your time.

Needs TLC - supposed to mean needs Tender Loving Care, but what it really means is needs Time, Labor, and Cash. Avoid like the plague.

Negotiable - means that the owner is willing to go lower than the price stated.

Original - you see this word a lot in ads for older vehicles. A car that's "all original" or in "original condition" has all the original parts from the engine down to the doormats. Anything that has been removed, lost, or broken should have been replaced with an original part.

Original Owner or **One Owner** - means that the car has had the same owner since new. These are the ones to look for. One owner means less chance for abuse.
Runs Excellent - self-explanatory.
Runs Good - doesn't run excellent.
Runs - basically means the engine runs, but is on its last leg. If you see an ad that says "runs," run away from it.
Sedan - a 2- or 4-door hard-top auto with a trunk.

Keep in mind, the prices you see advertised are padded. It doesn't mean the seller will actually get that. So consider this: If you have $2,000 to buy a new car and you see many '86s of the model you want selling in the $2,200 to $2,500 range, then you are right in the ball park. You can always count on sellers increasing the price of their autos hundreds above what they would actually take. We'll discuss this in detail in the negotiation chapter. In the meantime, don't let over-priced cars in a certain year lead you to believe that you can't afford one.

For those of us who live in a small town where there isn't much of a used car market, all this can be difficult to do. But if there's a larger city an hour or two away, it would be a good idea to check out the market there. You can do this without driving there if the city's paper and auto publications are available in your town. When it comes time to go look at cars, it could be well worth the one-or two-hour trip to find a decent car at a reasonable price. If you don't already have one, this would be a good time to get a city street map to make it easier to find your way around.

FINANCING

The best way to buy a car is with a lump-sum of cash. However, if you don't have the money saved up in a nest or have a rich uncle to schmooze, you'll be at the bank's mercy and must borrow--like the rest of us. If such is the case, financing becomes a big part of your research. Find out up front how much car you can afford and get pre-approved with a finance company that offers a competitive Annual Percentage Rate (APR). This way you will know how much the loan will cost you, the amount of your monthly payment, and the length of term BEFORE you go used car shopping. Finding an auto loan that fits you is like finding a car that fits you; you have to shop around. Some loan companies offer better deals than others.

The best way to finance your car is through a home equity loan. If you're a homeowner, check with your bank to see if you have enough equity to finance the amount you need for a car. The advantage in doing this allows you to deduct the interest payments at the end of the year, whereas in a conventional auto loan you can not.

If you belong to an employee credit union, this would also be an excellent source to check for low rates. If you don't own a home or belong to a credit union, find the best rate you can through the commercial banks and get yourself set up with one.

Most banks and finance companies like to see 20% down (depending on the year of the car) on a used car loan. If you can come up with more, it is to your advantage. I recommend putting down as much as you can and financing as little as possible. It will mean lower monthly payments or a shorter term and, most importantly, less interest to pay in the long run.

AUTO INSURANCE

Insurance is expensive these days, thanks to frauds and ambulance-chasing lawyers convincing accident victims to sue for outrageous sums for their "pain and suffering." And with a $30,000 car not an uncommon thing these days, the rising cost of autos has also contributed to the steep premiums we all pay.

If you are a first-time car buyer or making a drastic change from your previous auto, like going from a pickup truck to a sports car, you better get an estimate on insurance BEFORE you buy. Most of us do not like surprises and you may be surprised, unpleasantly, after you purchase that 'Vette and find yourself short when you go to insure it.

The best place to start checking for good rates would be through your homeowner's insurance policy--if you're a homeowner, that is. If not, find out which company your parents are with. Most agencies will offer family discounts on auto insurance policies.

Otherwise, the only other advice I can give here is to shop around. Surf the yellow pages and dial until your finger goes numb. Not all insurance agencies are created equal, as you will find when you receive a wide range of quotes. Go with the lowest from a reputable company.

THE EIGHT GOLDEN RULES OF RESEARCH

1) Focus on at least two models that suit your needs
2) Read up on them at the library, finding out as much as possible
3) Get the book price quotes from the Blue Book and *Edmunds* or a similar price guide
4) Touch base with a couple of mechanics for future inspections
5) Study the classified ads and learn the market on the cars you seek
6) Get your finances in order
7) Know what insurance will cost
8) Never be in a hurry to buy a used car

CHAPTER 2:
THE SEARCH

ARE YOU READY?

Have you narrowed your focus down to two or three particular models? Do you know which features you want? Do you know what the wholesale and retail prices are in a Blue Book and *Edmunds*? Did you read every auto classified publication you could get your hands on to learn what the going market is on the year models you desire? Did you get yourself lined up with at least one reliable mechanic? Is your financing all set to go at a moment's notice? Did you call and get some quotes from several insurance agents? Have you read my book all the way through, made notes accordingly, and understood clearly what is being presented? If you have, your research is complete. You are now ready to start the search.

Because you've already been scanning the ads, you know where to look for possible leads. By this time you should already know on which days weekly publications come out. Make a point to get the publication as soon as it's published. If a particular auto seller comes out every Friday, you don't want to be in town picking up a copy on Thursday. The ads are already a week old, and you will find that many cars have already sold. Quite often people sell cars well below market value because they are in dire need for some quick cash or they don't realize their car's full worth.

Remember, the dealers read the same ads and are constantly hunting for a kill. You are not hunting for a kill, but you are hunting for a reasonable deal--and sometimes even those go quickly.

INTERPRETING AN AD

Let's say you are looking for a Honda Accord and you come across a classified ad which reads:

> **'89 Honda Accord LX** - 4 dr,
> 5spd, low mi, looks and runs
> like new $6,800 call 555-5555

Now, because you have done your research, you know the LX is the luxury edition with all the goodies. What you don't know is how many miles the car has or it's real condition. Even though the ad says "low miles," your idea of low miles for an '89 might not be the same as that of the seller's. "Looks and runs like new" also sounds good, but again, your idea of something that looks and runs like new may not coincide with the seller's.

I once looked at a car which supposedly "looked like new" that had been hit in the rear fender. When I questioned the seller about his misleading ad, this was his reply: "Except for the dent, everything looks like new. Just look at that interior, not even a crack in the dash!"

The price of $6,800 is reasonable because you know what the fair market value of an '89 Accord is, thanks to your research. This ad is worth a phone call and that's something that takes only two seconds to decide.

QUESTIONS TO ASK

When you call, greet the owner politely and always reread the ad back to him. "I'm calling about the Accord. That's an '89 LX?..." Get into the habit of doing this just to double check that there hasn't been a misprint on the paper's behalf. You wouldn't want to drive an hour to look at what you thought was going to be an '89 Accord and have it turn out to be a '79.

"How many miles are on it?" would be the next question to ask. You can figure about 12,000 to 15,000 miles a year is average. The '89, being six years old, should have less than 72,000 miles if the ad said low miles. Always ask this question whether the ad says anything about mileage or not. Mileage is a key indicator of how much wear is on the engine. If the car's been properly maintained, we can assume the less miles on it, the more life it has left. But if an engine has been rebuilt or replaced, then the mileage doesn't apply.

Keep in mind, any car with a new or rebuilt engine that isn't more than eight years old has either had a hard life or is a poor design to begin with, and you didn't complete your research. In either case, stay away. Other costly repairs are just around the corner.

"How long have you owned it?" A very important question. If the person has owned it since new, then you are speaking to the original owner. Originally owned cars are highly desired over multiple-owner cars. Why? A multiple owner-car is more likely to have been neglected by an uncaring owner at some point in its life. How would you know for sure if the oil was changed on schedule or if the engine was properly tuned?

With multiple owners, you'll never know for sure about the car's past, but with an original owner, you'll be able to find out about the whole life of the car. That's not to say that all originally owned cars have been well cared for, but if they weren't, you'll know as soon as you see the car. Years of neglect will be staring you in the face.

In all the single-owner cars I have come across I can't recall one that was in bad shape. I guess original owners are just a special breed. They buy a brand new car with the intention of keeping it for a long time, so they take good care of it. A one-owner car is what you want. It's what the dealers want. It's what everybody wants.

If the owner has not owned it since new, ask if he bought it from the original owner. He may be the second or even third owner and know the previous owner(s) and what they were like. These are the kinds of things you like to hear when calling about used cars.

If it turns out that the owner has only had the car for a short period and doesn't know how many previous owners there were, then we are looking at a car blind. You can still buy a decent car blindly, you just have to be extra careful about it. A car that has changed a lot of hands may have something wrong with it that is expensive to fix. Which leads us to our next question.

"Why are you selling it?" Always assume that people are selling cars because there's something wrong with them. I know this seems like a paranoid way of thinking, but I want you to think this way to protect yourself. Many people will own a car until the engine starts leaking or the clutch starts slipping or the tires wear out or a combination of problems start adding up.

Instead of fixing the problem(s), they decide to buy a new car and let the next owner deal with it. Why put money into their car if they are about to sell it anyway? But in order to get the best price they will try to hide the car's faults and THEY WILL LIE TO YOU ABOUT THEIR CAR'S CONDITION. So don't believe what they say. Believe what your common sense and your mechanic say.

People can always lie about why they're selling their car, but more times than not you'll be able to detect if they're being honest with you. This is a question you'll ask twice: once over the phone and once when you look at the car. Notice if the second response differs from the first. If possible, try and ask a different person the second time to see if his or her answers coincide. For example, ask the wife over the phone the first time, and the husband in person the second time, etc.

People have all kinds of reasons to sell a car. The ones we like to hear are, "I'm selling it because I just bought a new car." Rather than trade in their used model to a dealer, many owners choose to sell their cars privately because they can get more money on their own. Remember, dealers are going to mark up a trade-in to make a profit, so they can only offer so much, which is well below market value. The new-car excuse is the one you'll most likely hear from an original owner.

Another good reason which can also give you some bargaining muscle is if someone is moving. These people may be desperate, especially if their phones aren't ringing. So keep your eyes peeled for "moving, must sell" ads. Sometimes people come into a tight money situation and, for one reason or another, they need to liquidate their car for cash. They are having a baby or they got laid off. Whatever the reason, as long as it's justified, you can rest easy when it's a person problem and not a car problem.

If the seller says he's bought something else, which is also used, it may be just his personal taste, but it could also be because the car has been nothing but a money pit and he needs to unload it. Other excuses to be nervous about are ones like "I don't need it anymore" or "I want to upgrade." Any excuse with this type of tone is a good indication of a car that people are unhappy with, so be wary.

"Is everything working" or "Is there anything broken that needs to be fixed?" These are good questions to ask. Today, cars are loaded up with so much power gadgetry you want to know if everything is working properly ahead of time (cruise control, air-conditioning, power windows, etc.).

Even though you'll double check all this stuff when you inspect the car, ask up front anyway. If something is broken you can call the dealership ahead of time and get a phone estimate for the MAXIMUM amount it could cost to fix. Then, if you decide to make an offer on the car, you use this repair cost as bargaining leverage.

"Has the car ever been in an accident?" People can easily lie about this one, but there are ways to look for hidden body damage that we will discuss later. If an owner admits to a fender bender over the phone, ask for the details. If the car has just been bumped slightly with only minor damage, then it's still worth a look.

However, if the car has had major damage, stay away. Once a car's frame has been bent it is very difficult to get it back to the way it was. Cars that have been hit commonly have alignment problems that are unrepairable. The end result may be tires wearing out much too fast, rough cornering, and steering wheel shimmy.

"Are you negotiable in your price?" Always ask this over the phone. Most of the time the response will be something like "I'll negotiate a little" or "Yes, I need to sell it." Judging by the way they answer can tip you off as to how low an offer you dare make.

If you've read my definitions, then you know that ads which read "firm" mean the seller doesn't want to budge on the price, but don't let this stop you from making an offer a couple of hundred dollars less. Firm to some people means they'll only sell their car two hundred less rather than five hundred. It never hurts to ask. The worst thing that could happen is that they say no. The best thing that could happen is that you save yourself a couple of Ben Franklins. You'd be surprised how many times it has worked for me.

"Has anyone else looked at it yet?" and **"How long have you had it for sale?"** Like all the other questions, people can lie about these too. But if the owner seems honest this far in your conversation, ask if anyone else has seen the car yet. What we want to hear is "No, you'll be the first." This means that the car on the market is a virgin and you are in line for a first look. Why is this good?

A car that has been on the market for a week or longer and had three or more lookers indicates that either there's something wrong with it or the car is over-priced. If a car has had one or two people look at it and pass, it's still worth a look. They could have just been a couple of looky-loos who really weren't ready to buy or are having financing problems, etc. But when you get up to three or more previous lookers and the car still hasn't sold, it's almost a guarantee that there is something wrong with it.

If you have some extra time, go have a look. And be careful. When you go to inspect it, keep asking yourself this question: "Why hasn't this car sold yet?"

OTHER QUESTIONS TO ASK

"How much are you asking?" Even if the ad states their price in bold letters, ask this question anyway. Their response can give you clues to how negotiable they are. "I'm asking $5,500, but open to offers," "The price in the ad is $4,300, but I'd probably take $4,000". This is a form of preconditioning in which I go into detail in the **Negotiation** chapter.

If there isn't a price stated in the ad then you definitely want the answer to this before making an appointment. Don't let someone play games with you on this either. Sometimes people will try to get you to come out and look first, then talk price. If anyone tries this with you, just tell them you're not coming over until you know what their asking price is.

"Do you have any service records or receipts for work done to the car?" If they do, ask them to have them available for you to look at when you come over. Also ask if any major repairs have been performed like brakes, clutch, etc.

"Who did the maintenance?" If the seller did his own oil changes, ask if he kept a ledger or service record. If he did, ask to have it available for you to see as well. If he didn't, don't believe him when he tells you he changed the oil every 3,000 miles. I say this with confidence because the type of people who change their oil every 3,000 miles are not the type of people who don't make record of it.

"Does the car have a salvage title?" If the car seems bargain priced, nine times out of ten this is the reason. Nothing's worse than putting in the time and effort to find a car, only to learn that it has a salvage title right before you are about to transfer ownership. For more information on what a salvage title is, turn to page 82. But you can trust me right here and now. You don't want to buy a car with a salvage title. You want a car with a clean title.

"Are you the owner?" If the person selling the car is not the owner, suspect that the seller is a dealer, at least a part-time one, probably selling cars one at a time from his house. If this is the case, be extra careful when checking over the car and don't believe a word he says. He may have bought it at an auction or from someone out of the paper the week before and knows nothing about the car's history, even though he may tell you he is selling it for his "cousin," who took excellent care of it.

Listen to how the seller talks. Does he seem pretty smooth with what he is saying like he's done this many times before, or does he sound awkward and unsure of himself? If he seems well rehearsed, figure him to be a dealer. Call your local motor vehicle department to see if there are any additional forms you or the seller must fill out when a third party is involved in the transfer of title.

GET AN APPOINTMENT

If you decide the car is worth a look, set up an appointment to see the car as soon as possible. Within an hour is preferable. I know this is impossible for most, because of work and all, but try to arrange it so when you are calling on used car ads you have time to go and look as soon as you hang up the phone.

Consider the following scenarios: You come home from work on Friday with the latest auto seller publication. You scan through the ads and find a car you've been looking for. You don't wait until tomorrow to call because dinner is at 7 p.m. and after that it'll be too late. You're going to call right now. You talk to the person for about 15 minutes, drilling him with questions, and everything sounds good so far. You tell him you want to come look at it now, and he agrees to meet with you in an hour.

You get there 15 minutes early with $50 to $100 (or your checkbook) in your pocket. You spend about 45 minutes to inspect and test drive the car. Everything seems okay. You negotiate a fair price with the understanding that you want to have your mechanic check it out first thing tomorrow morning (much more on this later). You leave a $50 deposit which will be refunded if the car doesn't pass your mechanic's inspection. Should your mechanic find only minor problems, you will be allowed to either pass or renegotiate to a lower price with the seller. You come home late for dinner, excited and hungry.

The next morning you meet at your mechanic's shop, where he carefully inspects it. Except for some brakes that will soon need replacing, everything checks out. You're ready to buy the car as is, but because of the brakes, you try to bargain him down further in price. The owner, who saw the report from the mechanic, agrees and you save yourself more money and end up with a car that lets you sleep peacefully at night.

For those of you who must drive to a nearby city, the situation is slightly different. You are setting up two or more appointments for first thing Saturday morning. You want to make it worthwhile to make that drive, and hopefully you'll only need to give up a couple of Saturdays until you score.

This is how cars are bought. You have to absorb some inconveniences in your personal life, like missing dinner or giving up your weekend, but with some time and effort, you will be rewarded. Isn't this how most things work in life?

EXCUSES, EXCUSES

That's what you'll need to escape from some of the clunkers you will find yourself looking at. No matter how well you screen them over the phone, you will still get stuck looking at a "beater." But a good excuse gets you out of there quickly and politely. Whether you just started looking or have been looking for months, don't go car shopping without a good excuse for a quick escape.

- "I just started looking, and I want to see what else is around before I make any decisions."
- "I have two others to look at, and I want to see those before I make any decisions."

What you don't want to do is upset someone by telling him what you really think of his car. Call it diplomacy, call it lying, but in a gun-happy society where people shoot you for looking at them wrong, I call it surviving.

For telephone excuses, don't tell someone you're coming over to look at his car when you have no intentions of doing so. I find many people do this just to get off the phone. There's nothing more rude than telling someone you'll be there at a certain time and then not showing. You're wasting their time, and they may be scheduling appointments with serious buyers around yours. Have the decency to tell them you're not interested when you're really not. If you're afraid of hurting someone's feelings, you can always say:

- "You know, I really wanted an automatic," or "You know, I really wanted a five-speed." In other words, whatever their car has, you wanted the opposite.
- "It doesn't sound like what I want. I'm going to have to pass."

If you talk to someone on the phone who seems real anxious to sell you his car and you can tell already that it's not something you want, use the excuse I use.

- "I have a couple other ads that I want to call before I start setting up any appointments. I'll call you back when I'm ready to come by."

There's something about eager beaver sellers. The more anxious they are to get me over there, the more I don't want to go. It usually means there's something wrong with their car, and they will try some fast talking to keep from losing you. Lose them instead.

CARS WITH OUT-OF-STATE PLATES

I see it all the time. A car with an out-of-state plate selling for a bargain price. But there's usually a reason why. If you're considering a car from out of state, you'd better find out exactly what the registration and/or emission regulations are in your home state BEFORE you purchase.

Here in California, where emissions are very strict, we have what is known as a smog impact fee for out-of-state vehicles. The fee is $300 and there's no way around it if you want to register the car in California. On top of that is the smog inspection. If the out-of-state car had any emission components removed that are required here in California, but not required in the state from which the car originated, you will have to put them back on, no matter what the cost. This could get into lots of dough. Vehicles from out of state may also need special attention for rust or flood damage.

Other states may have similar fees for registering out-of-state vehicles, so if you're on a really tight budget it would be wise to find this out in advance. Call your motor vehicle department or state certified inspection center (if your state has them) and ask. All they need to know is the year of the model you wish to register, and they can tell you what the requirements were for that year. Don't forget to add any extra registration charges to your bargaining list.

This is just one of those things you want to be aware of when used car shopping. It's a good idea for California residents to find a mechanic who also does smog inspections so he can make sure everything is up to snuff. You don't want any surprises later.

CITY MILES VS. FREEWAY MILES

Here in California, where you must drive the freeways to get anywhere, it's common to find cars approaching the 200,000 mile mark that are still running fine. At the same time, it's possible to find cars that were driven primarily in city traffic, such as a delivery service, etc., which require engine work before reaching 90,000 miles. Considering both vehicles receive the same service intervals, why does one engine easily outlast the other?

It's simple. Most engine wear occurs during cold engine start-up and through frequent stop-and-go driving. Cars that are driven on the freeway at constant speeds experience minimal engine wear. Look at it this way: A person who does a daily freeway round trip of 50 miles only cold starts his engine twice and drives a few stop-and-go miles to and from the freeway. Whereas, a delivery driver who services a 50-mile route will start his engine dozens of times, and be subject to stop-and-go traffic during the entire route.

If a car you're looking at has high miles and you can verify that they are mostly freeway miles, don't let it keep you from buying. But watch out for cars that were subject to city driving, no matter how many miles they may have.

DON'T BE HASTY

If you ever get frustrated in your search and become tempted to take the used car dealership route, here are some things you should consider. Used car dealers get many of their cars from auto auctions. Have you ever wondered where the auctions get these cars?

Some come from businesses that were used for delivery fleets. Some come from car rental agencies who unload them after a certain number of miles to avoid costly repairs. Some are repossessions that come from banks who are trying to cut their losses on defaulted loans by irresponsible owners. If someone wasn't responsible enough to make his payments, do you think he was responsible enough to service his car regularly? In each case you're looking at cars that either have a) high miles; b) been driven hard; c) been neglected; or d) all of the above.

In addition, dealers will go to these auctions and listen to cars run but won't drive them. Because you can't find out about a transmission problem, or a clutch that's about to go out, or an irreparable alignment that wears down a 40,000 mile tire in 8,000 miles by listening to the engine, it's common for dealers to get stuck with a dog. Now, what do you suppose they are going to do with those dogs? You don't think a dealer is going to absorb a loss, do you? He's going to pass it on to you.

Don't forget that dealers also buy autos right out of the classifieds from private parties and then turn around and sell them for much more. These are cars that are available to you just as easy as they are to them. The difference is you could save hundreds up front on the purchase price and possibly thousands later in costly repairs when you buy from a private party.

Even though most new car dealerships who take trade-ins may have some decent used cars on their lot, you won't find any at a reasonable price. Dealers work off commissions, and they know the market. They are into making money, and you won't get too far with them at the negotiation table. So only take the dealership route as a last resort.

DANGLING CARROTS

One last thing: In your travels through the classifieds you may see dealers advertising cars at unbelievably low prices or financing offers that sound too good to be true. That's usually because they are. Dealers play con games to get you onto their lot.

The old "bait and switch" is a favorite. In the paper you see Honest John's Used Cars is advertising a certain car for a really low price. Frustrated with the classifieds, you go down to check it out. When you inquire about the ad car you'll hear something like, "We just sold it an hour ago, but we have these similar models over here that just came in." You can bet your sweet bippi they won't be for the same price, though.

With the financing carrot, you see an advertisement from Crazy Joe's Deals on Wheels that claims zero down with 100% percent financing at only 4.9% interest. Now you say to yourself, "That's much better than buying a car through my bank," so you race down to Crazy Joe's to inquire about the ad and a friendly salesman acknowledges and starts showing you around. You find a car you like and test drive it while the salesman assures you what a great deal you'll be getting. You want the car, and you go into the sales office (shark pit) to negotiate and close the deal.

If you're not paying attention it may go right over your head, but if you're on your toes you notice the 4.9% interest has somehow grown to 12%. So you stop him and ask about the ad, and you get something like, "Oh, that's just for first-time buyers," or "It's just for senior citizens," or "It's for people with excellent credit," or "It's for people with no credit." Are you starting to catch on?

Whatever your situation is, the 4.9% loan will be for those with the opposite features. In reality, the 4.9% deal just doesn't exist. It's just a hook. And now you are hooked because you find this out after having spent hours inspecting, test driving, and negotiating a price with the dealer. By this time you want the car bad and you're not about to let a couple of silly interest points stand in you way. This is just another one of the many ways the dealer can get you--hook, line, and sinker. So the moral of the dealer story is, if it sounds too good to be true, it is.

THE SEVEN GOLDEN RULES OF THE SEARCH

1) Read the ads religiously
2) Know the right questions to ask
3) Learn how to interpret their responses
4) Set up an appointment as soon as possible
5) Memorize polite excuses
6) Avoid dealers like the plague
7) Never be in a hurry to buy a used car

CHAPTER 3:

CHECKING OUT THE BEAST

The first time you read this chapter, just read through and go with the flow. There's no way I expect you to remember all this stuff, which is why I have included an inspection checklist in Appendix B (page 168). Before you go car hunting, make some photocopies for your reference. This will help you to remember all those steps and keep you from overlooking anything.

When you have made an appointment to look at your first car, go with the thought in mind that it won't be your last. The chances that you buy the first car you look at are unlikely, unless you didn't listen to what I wrote and get swept off your feet by your favorite color.

SOME FIRSTHAND TIPS

When looking at used cars, wear clothes you don't mind getting dirty. You'll be poking around the engine and getting down on your knees as well. And bring a rag, too. You'll most likely get some grease on your fingers.

Always show up 15-30 minutes before the time you had set. If they say come over at 3 o'clock, you show up between 2:30 and

2:45. Why do this? Because you want to see if they are adding fresh oil or wiping up oil drops from the garage floor or adding air to that slow-leaking tire or running the car and driving it around because it starts better when warmed up. You get the picture? By showing up early, sometimes you can catch them in the act of hiding something they don't want you to know about.

Also, make it a point to look at a car during the day. You want to see what a car's paint and body look like in the daylight, not under artificial light or in poor lighting. Things just don't look the same under artificial lighting. Many people I know, myself included, have bought autos that were inspected at night only to find the morning sun revealing some body waves that we could have sworn weren't there the night before.

If you're looking at cars during the winter months when it gets dark early, you could inspect them on weekends or maybe slip away from your job during lunch hour to have a look. If you do look at night and you like the car, look at it once more in the daylight before closing the deal. You may be glad you did.

Always make it a point to look at a car with a cold engine. First thing in the morning would be the optimum time, but I know this isn't always possible. The reason for this is that you want to see how the car starts on a cold engine. Is the choke in adjustment, or does the engine cough and stall?

Most importantly, listen for worn lifters. While the engine is cold, worn lifters will be talking to you loud and clear with a terrible knocking sound coming from the top of the engine. But once oil circulates and has a chance to coat the lifters, the sound becomes deadened and magically disappears. This can even slip by your mechanic, since you warm up the engine driving to his shop. Replacing eight lifters on a 4-cylinder motor can run $300, so request a cold engine before you go over to look.

And one last note: Bring a flashlight. Even during the day, you need a flashlight to check the engine for oil seepage, and you will want to look around underneath the car as well. You should already carry a flashlight in your car for emergencies, so if you don't, now is a good time to get one. If you do keep one in your car, make sure it's working properly BEFORE you go used car shopping.

A WORD ABOUT COLOR

Color is the last thing to consider when buying a used car, but it is a consideration. You don't have to be Einstein to understand that, especially in the summer, darker colors make a car hotter than lighter colors. What most people don't realize, however, is that darker colors, especially black, show dirt more, whereas lighter colors, especially white, make dirt invisible.

How can this be? It's simple. Light colors reflect light and dark colors absorb light. When dirt and dust settle on a white car and the sun is beating down reflecting a light-colored surface, the dirt becomes practically invisible to the eye. But when dirt and dust settle on a black surface, the color of the dirt will be easily reflected from the sun absorbing color. That's why it's so hard to keep a black car clean.

It is preferable to buy a used car with its original paint job, which should be the case for any car up to ten years old. I'd rather buy a ten-year-old car that needs a paint job than a ten-year-old car that has just been painted.

Why? Because with an original paint job I know exactly where the body's at with rust, accidents, etc., whereas with the new paint job, I can only guess. If there were some small rust holes in the body and the car had been worked on by professionals, you and I won't know where the holes were for at least another year until the rust starts to bubble back through. You see, once rust has eaten a hole in your car it can never be stopped, it can only be slowed down. New paint scares me. It usually means a car that's been in an accident or has serious rust, neither of which I want.

One more thing, avoid color-changed cars. If the car has been repainted, you want the color to be the same as that of the original. If the paint is a custom color, the car loses value. Why? Because most people are turned off by custom colors. So even though you think that pink VW looks cool, keep in mind when it's your turn to sell, you'll find out just how unique you are when countless people pass on it, and you're forced to lower the price well below market value.

HOW TO CHECK FOR BODY DAMAGE FROM AN ACCIDENT

Three of the simplest ways for revealing evidence of a car that has been either the hitter or hittee is by checking for overspray and mismatched paint, eyeballing a car's body and seams, and inspecting the car's frame.

Although it's no guarantee, most repainted cars are repainted because the owner received a check on his insurance claim from an accident. Think about it. Cars are rarely painted because someone has an extra $1,500 laying around and they suddenly want a new gloss.

Look closely for overspray around all the window seals and lights and other trim. If the car was repainted, it usually doesn't take long to find where the tape didn't cover a sliver of the window seal, indicating new paint. Another good place to check for overspray is in the engine compartment. If the car had a color change, you may find its original color here. With your flashlight handy, look at the wheel wells alongside the engine and the fire wall (behind the engine). Look for overspray on wires and hoses. The trunk is another place to look if you suspect a color change. Pull up the floor mat in the trunk and you will see the car's original color. Weather stripping around the doors and trunk will usually catch a little overspray, revealing new paint.

Mismatched paint is a definite indication of a car that's been in an accident. This is where a car has had some body parts replaced, such as a fender and hood, and then just the new parts get sprayed with the original color. Only problem is, a car that is a few years old is going to have sun-faded, ozone-oxidized paint that won't be as deep in color or as shiny as the new body parts. Mismatched paint is difficult to notice at night, which is why you should look at a car in broad daylight. To make sure that all fenders, doors, and hoods match, you need to look at the car from all angles in the sun and in the shade without your sunglasses.

While you're doing this you can check for body waves, which will also indicate an accident. To check for waves in the body, park your eyes about three feet in front of the headlight and look down the length of the car. The front fender, doors, and rear fender should all line up straight as an arrow. Look at both sides. If you notice any waves in the sheet metal, the car has been hit. However, don't confuse body waves with door pings. A door ping will look like a dimple in the sheet metal, whereas body waves are more broad. Check the roof for body waves too. If you find any, the car has either been rolled or someone walked on the roof and dented it.

Have you ever seen that commercial for the Lexus where they roll the ball bearing down the seam that separates the fender from the hood? They are trying to impress you with the precision of a well-built car by illustrating its perfectly matching joints. This is what you will be looking at when you're checking for hidden body damage. I'm not saying to carry a marble with you to roll down the seams; don't embarrass yourself. It's easy enough just to eyeball them.

The places to look are where the hood, trunk, and doors open. With them all closed, check these seams carefully. The gap should run evenly all the way around. If you come across a seam that is wide at one end and narrow at the other, then you are looking at a car that has been hit. Question the owner about this and if he denies it was in an accident or claims he bought it that way, he is either lying or it was hit when it was with the previous owner.

If the owner admits to an accident, get the details. How much damage was there and what was replaced? Who did the body repairs? If you are looking at uneven seams, open and close the trunk or door that is in question to see how freely it works. A sticking door or a trunk that is hard to close is further evidence of a car that's been hit. If this is combined with mismatched paint, then give this car an automatic failure. However, if the seams are only a little off, nothing's sticking, and the paint matches, continue to the next step, which is checking the frame.

To check the frame, you need to get down on your hands and knees with your trusty flashlight and shine it on the underbelly of the car. The frame will be the thickest gauge metal going up and down the full length of the car, usually on both sides (depending on the car). You want to pay particular attention to this, shining your light on it all the way up and down. Check it from under both sides of the car. You're looking for anything that doesn't look right, like metal that is bent or weld marks which basically looks like melted metal. If you see something like I've just described, then, congratulations, you have verified that the car has been in an accident. AUTOMATIC FAILURE! My advice here is to quietly leave. It's not worth the gamble, buying something and hoping it is back to normal. Once a car's frame has been messed with, it may never be the same.

If everything looks okay then continue with your inspection. Please remember, even if you do miss evidence of an accident, your mechanic will catch it and can decipher its seriousness.

Another suspect for an accident, and this goes for rust as well, is one door lock that requires a different key. Most cars are made with one key that fits all locks. Check the trunk and all door locks with the ignition key. If any lock doesn't work, suspect that that door or trunk lid has been replaced. Please note that some cars come with a separate key for the trunk. Find out up front if this is the case for those cars you seek.

Unhidden body damage is easy to find because its unsightliness stares you right in the face. And, because you knew what questions to ask over the phone, you have hopefully weeded out the undesirables. But sometimes people exaggerate, fib, or lie right through their teeth, and that small dent in the fender turns out to be bashed so bad that the trunk lid has to be tied down. Of course, at this point you want to strangle the person for bringing you here and wasting your time. If this should happen, grin and bear it, and politely tell them that that wasn't what you had in mind, and move on.

HOW TO CHECK FOR BODY DAMAGE FROM RUST

Unless you live near the ocean, rust isn't much of a problem here in the arid southwest. However, in the north, where they salt the roads in the winter, or in the coastal southeast, where the combination of humidity and salt air practically melts your car away, rust can be a big obstacle in used car hunting.

Rust usually starts in one of two ways. It either starts from the exterior, such as a chip in your paint exposing bare metal or, worse yet, comes from the inside and starts bubbling up through the paint. Rust that comes from the inside out is a sign of a poorly made car, but any car that is visually rusty should be avoided.

Even if you figure in the cost of body work and a paint job, once a rust hole has started it can never be stopped, only slowed down. Rust never sleeps, and usually within a year it will start bubbling back through, depreciating your car's resale value radically. If you live in a "rust belt" region, be wary of older cars that have been recently repainted. You can hide a lot of sin with body filler and paint. It is up to you to detect it.

In checking for rust, it makes sense to look in the most common problem areas. This would be around the wheel wells and the fenders immediately behind the tires where stones get kicked up, chip the paint, and expose bare metal for rust to attack. The front of the car can also catch flying stones from other cars, making this a problem area as well.

With your trusty flashlight in hand, look underneath the car behind the front and rear tires on both sides. Of course, before you do this MAKE SURE THE CAR IS PARKED ON A LEVEL SURFACE IN PARK/GEAR AND THE EMERGENCY BRAKE ENGAGED! If it's on a slope, put blocks under the wheels for added safety. Shine your light on the inside of the fenders as well as the wheel wells. You are looking for excess body filler, which from this side looks like hardened putty all globbed up.

In areas where you don't have a clear view, use your fingers as your eyes and feel around. Do you feel globs of hardened putty under there? Other rust-prone places to check would be the exterior flooring under the driver's and passenger's seats, under the carpeting/matting on the floor inside, under the carpeting/matting in the trunk, and around the engine compartment. USE YOUR FLASHLIGHT, YOUR EYES AND YOUR FINGERS!

Another way of checking areas is by using your ears. Above the area in question, tap lightly on the car's body with your knuckles. You should hear a tinny metal sound. Continue tapping and move slowly down to the area in question. Does the sound change from tinny to solid and dense? If it does, then that's further evidence of body filler and it's decision-making time for you. Would you want this car providing everything else checks out? The car may look great now, but if it looks like hell in a year, you'll be the loser in this deal.

If he hasn't already told you, ask the seller who did the body work. If he plays dumb--his car receives an automatic failure. However, if he has receipts from a well-known body shop, get the name of the shop and the person who did the body work. You need to find out how the rust was addressed. Was it ground down or completely cut away?

The grinding/sanding method is the least expensive and, consequently, most common way rust is repaired. If the rust is caught before it creates a hole in the metal, then, yes, it can be stopped. The rust is sanded away until it is bare, shiny metal, then primed and painted.

Unfortunately, most people don't notice rust on their car until it is too late. Large rust spots turn into rust holes once they face the sand blaster. After that, you are fighting a losing battle because body filler with paint on top is only a temporary solution to a permanent problem.

Yet because people want to sell their cars for the most money and the cost is relatively cheap, they get the economy paint job, which is just enough to make it look good. Or worse yet, some people will attempt the body work themselves. Trust me on this: You don't want to buy a car that looks good temporarily.

However, contrary to what you just read, there are ways to beat rust. But they are very costly and usually only used as a last-ditch effort to save a car from the auto graveyard. Such is the case on many classic car restorations.

The best way to cure a car of rust is simply by replacing that rusty fender, door, etc. with a new or rust-free salvaged part from the junkyard. Of course, if the rust has spread to the main part of the body, you're left with the second and less desirable cure: cutting out the rusty metal and welding in new pieces. The metal is then ground down and smoothed out with body filler.

When done right, the body will last just as long as it would new, and a professional can make it invisible. So if you were able to contact the body shop that worked on the car and know for a fact that the car in question was corrected in this manner, then continue on with your inspection.

TIRES AND SUSPENSION

Take a close look at all four tires. You will find information about the tire's size and type written right on its sidewalls. They should all be the same. There shouldn't be three 195s and one 225, and there should never be a mixture of radials and bias ply tires. You may see a car with a matched pair of tires on the front and a slightly larger matched pair on the rear. This is okay for now, but later you'll want to install the correct tire size for maximum safety and performance (check the owner's manual or the dealer for this information). If this is the case, figure in the cost for two new tires.

To check the tread, stick a key between the grooves in the most worn area of the tire. Put your thumb nail flush up to the tread and against the key, then remove. Anything 1/8 inch or less will require new tires within 5,000 miles. That translates to less than four months for the average driver. The cost of four new tires can run you anywhere from $200 to $500 depending on the size and quality. That's a big bill. Make a note on your checklist to find out the cost of new tires for this model. You want to keep this in mind when bargaining time comes around.

To test the shocks, go around to each corner of the car and push up and down a few times and then let go to see how much it bounces on its own. If it goes up and down more than twice, find out what the cost of a new set of shocks for this car will be and add that to your bargaining list.

To detect a suspension problem, park the car on a level surface, take a few steps back from each corner of the car, and squat. Does the car sit level or is one corner sagging? It's not a common thing to come across a car with a broken spring which would be the cause for the rear to sag, but if it's a front corner sagging, you're looking at a possible bent frame or a tweaked front end. In either case, the car gets an automatic failure.

FLUIDS TO CHECK: OIL

To check the oil, the car must be on level ground for an accurate reading. Pull the dipstick out and wipe it clean with your rag. Reinsert and remove. The oil should be between the high mark and the add-oil mark. Also, notice what color the oil is. The darker it is, the older it is. With your rag handy, get a dab to rub between your fingers. Does it feel gritty?

Grit could be ground up metal or dirt from oil that is long overdue for a change. Either way it's bad news. Dirty oil is a sign of an owner who doesn't take proper care of his car. Light-colored oil (about the color of honey) is oil that has been recently changed. Ask the seller when the oil was changed last and see if his response coincides with what you see. Now would be a good time ask how often the oil was changed.

If they haven't already offered, ask if they can provide you with some sort of maintenance schedule or ledger that they have been religiously following. What you want to see is a schedule where the car's oil was changed regularly every 3,000 miles. Even up to every 5,000 miles is acceptable, but when you get up to six, seven, or 10,000 miles, then you have an engine with excessive wear. So, the more frequent the oil changes, the less wear on the engine and the better off you'll be.

Another thing you want to check is under the oil filler cap. Unscrew it and take a look. If there's a light brown, foamy substance on the underside of the cap, it means water from your cooling system is getting into your engine which could be through a head gasket or cracked block. This is bad news. Likewise oil will be making its way into the cooling system. Keep this in mind when you inspect the radiator. Any coolant getting into the engine or oil getting into the radiator gets an automatic failure.

AUTOMATIC TRANSMISSION

Find the automatic transmission dipstick and pull it out. Some cars have two high and two low marks for when the engine is running and when it is not. Just as long as the fluid registers on the dipstick, we are more concerned with the color and smell of the fluid rather than the level. With your rag nearby, get some on your finger and take a sniff. It should not smell burnt and should be pink in color. If it's brown and burnt smelling, then you are looking at a car that will soon be needing a new transmission. This automatic transmission gets an automatic failure. Walk away.

COOLANT

Make sure the engine is cold by lightly touching the radiator cap. If it's hot, don't try to take it off or you'll be taking a steam bath, which isn't much fun. If it's warm, you can drape your rag over it and turn SLOWLY. If it's cold, no problem. Just push down and turn in the direction the arrow indicates.

Look inside the radiator. The fluid should be a yellowish-green color. If it is brown or rusty in color, then this is a sign of a car overdue for a radiator flush and, hence, a car that is not being properly maintained. If it's clear, the car's cooling system has been drained and refilled with nothing but water, or is leaking and the owner just keeps adding water. In either case, this is a big no-no. New radiators can get pricey. Make a note for your mechanic, and he can give you an estimate later.

Most cars today come with a reservoir tank for the radiator. It is usually a plastic tank with a high and low mark on it. You can easily locate it by following the small hose that comes out from under the radiator cap to the unit. Make sure the fluid is between the marks and of the right color. Also, remember to check for any leaks before and after the test drive.

CHECK AIR FILTER, HOSES, AND BELTS

It's important to check the air cleaner to make sure it is in place. You wouldn't want to buy a car from some fool who has been driving around without one and allowing dust and dirt particles to wreak havoc on the cylinder walls. Plus, the clean or dirty filter will confirm the car's proper or improper maintenance. If the car's filter is in one of those confusing contraptions, leave it for your mechanic to check.

Visually check all hoses you come across on the engine. Even though they're inexpensive and easy enough to replace, you want to make sure they are all in apple pie order. There should be no cracked hoses with duct tape or electrical tape holding them together. Owners who do this are the ones you don't want to buy a car from. If they duct taped a $2.99 hose, you can imagine how long they went between oil changes.

CHECKING OUT THE BEAST   51

Fan belts, air-conditioning belts, alternator belts, etc., check them all. And before you go putting your hand down there, make sure the keys are not in the ignition and pull the center wire out from the distributor cap. That's that round thing with a bunch of thick wires that come from it and go to each spark plug. Pull the center one.

Using your flashlight, take a peak at the underside of the belt(s). The belt should be tight enough so that it just barely allows you to do this. Check them as much as your point of view will allow. Do the belts look cracked or frayed? If they do, you'll want to have new ones installed. Belts don't cost much, but they can be tricky to replace. Put down $30 per belt on your checklist which will cover labor as well.

THINGS TO LEAK OUT FOR

With your flashlight, check the engine block for oil seepage and leaks. Look all around on both sides. Does it coincide with the amount of miles on the odometer? The less miles on a car, the cleaner the engine should be. An engine with only 60,000 miles on it should have only some minor road grime, but don't freak out if there is some oily grime. As mileage starts to add up, most engines will seep a little oil from around the valve cover or the oil pan, yet it may still be a good running engine with plenty of spunk left in it.

So don't let this scare you, but do be afraid when you see WET oil seepage anywhere on the engine. This could be serious. Check the ground under where the car is parked. If you are in a spot where the car is usually parked, like the garage or driveway, notice how stained the ground is. If the car is parked in the street, then see if you notice any oil stains in their driveway or, if possible, in their garage. An oil stained driveway is more evidence of a car with a leakage problem.

Using your flashlight, look underneath the engine from the front as well as the right and left sides. An oily undercarriage is evidence of oil leaking while driving, and the wind is spraying it back. Look for fresh oil droplets under the engine and transmission. If you see droplets, ask the owner to start up the car (NOT WHILE YOU'RE UNDER THERE) to see if it starts dripping more.

Give the car a few minutes to get the oil circulating. If you notice steady oil dripping while the car is running, there could be a crack in the crankcase, a blown seal, or maybe someone simply forgot to tighten something down last time the car was worked on. Have the owner turn off the engine.

In the latter case, even though tightening something down could be easy enough to fix, you don't know how long the car has been like this or how many times the owner ran the oil down too low. Any car with steady oil dripping receives an automatic failure in my book. Don't take the risk. If there are fresh oil drops, but it doesn't drip while running, then continue with your inspection.

Whether this auto features a standard or automatic transmission, you'll want to have a look at its belly to see if it's leaking any fluid as well. Transmission leaks are not as common as engine oil leaks, but they do occur and, as long as you're under there with a flashlight looking for oil leaks, you may as well inspect the transmission too.

The transmission is bolted to the engine, usually directly behind it but not always. Many of the newer four-cylinder models are set sideways under the hood with a transaxle, making one compact mass of metal.

Shine the light on it and look for anything wet. It should be dry as a bone minus some road dirt. Automatic transmission fluid is pinkish-red, so if it is wet, touch it with your finger and verify that it is automatic transmission fluid and not oil. Vice versa when you are looking for oil leaks. Standard transmissions rarely leak, so make sure it is the transmission you are checking and not the engine. If the transmission is leaking gear oil (which looks like motor oil), let your mechanic make the diagnosis.

Other leaky things to watch for are radiator coolant and hydraulic brake/clutch fluid. Radiator coolant is greenish-yellow in color and mixed with water. If a car hasn't had a radiator flush in a long time, then the color would be closer to a rusty brown. If you see this kind of fluid under the radiator or engine, there could be a leaking water pump or a leaking radiator. Both puppies start in the $200 to $300 range and go up. But don't fail this car yet. Make a note for your mechanic, and he will give you an accurate diagnosis/estimate.

Hydraulic brake/clutch fluid is a clear oil-like substance with a strong smell. By looks, you could confuse it with new oil, but it has that strong odor which is hard to describe. So, next opportunity you have, use your own car, or your friend's if you don't have one, and familiarize yourself with it. Get a rag and find the master cylinder reservoir under the hood. Pop off the cap, get a dab on your finger, and take a whiff. Now you know what brake fluid smells like, and you won't confuse it with oil. By the way, don't get any on your clothes or the paint. It can do damage to both.

If you suspect a car is leaking brake fluid, step down firmly on the brake pedal. If the pedal goes down to the floor, don't drive the car. There is a major leak somewhere, and the brakes won't be working properly. The pedal should go down about halfway and stop. Keep the pressure on for a minute and see if it gives any more. If it does, there is a leak. If it doesn't, it's probably okay. If the brakes seem fine but you found some fluid, make a note and your mechanic can check it out later.

If you come across a car leaking hydraulic clutch fluid, it will either be coming from the master cylinder, which is mounted against the firewall under the hood, or from the slave cylinder that is mounted to the transmission. In the case of a leaking clutch master cylinder, it is possible for the fluid to drip inside the car. It would come down from behind the clutch pedal. Don't fail the car if you detect any leakage. It's not super expensive to replace the clutch master cylinder but, nonetheless, you have discovered more bargaining leverage. Make a note for your mechanic, and he can fill you in later.

CALIFORNIA EMISSIONS

California residents: there should be a sticker on the underside of the hood which declares that the vehicle meets federal AND State of California emission controls. That doesn't mean someone couldn't have later removed some smog control equipment, or the sticker for that matter, but this would be the place to start looking for clues. If the sticker says it meets only federal emission controls, then the car originated from out of state. Look for this sticker when checking out the car.

Another thing to check for is the gas filler tube. Open it up and make sure the inlet hasn't been modified to accept the larger leaded gas nozzle. If it has, then assume regular gas has been run through the engine and the catalytic converter is spent. If this is the case, the car won't pass smog until a new catalytic converter is replaced, which can cost upwards of $300. People have been known to do this in order to save on the cheaper gas at the pumps. If they were that cheap, imagine how often they changed their oil! Give this car an automatic failure.

As long as a car has all the required smog equipment, and the engine is in tune, it should pass the smog inspection with no problem. If a car fails smog with all the required emission equipment, and there's no evidence of tampering, the state has a cap on how much can be charged to correct it. For 1990 and newer vehicles, the cost can't be more than $300, for 1980-89 vehicles, not more than $175--and the cost decreases with age. Cars with repair estimates over the caps get waivered and, hence, a smog certificate.

THE TAIL PIPE

A car's tail pipe is one of the best ways to tell how an engine is running. Look inside the tail pipe and check the color. A normal running engine should be light gray to light brown. If the tail pipe isn't hot, run your finger around inside. Black sooty wet deposits indicate too rich a mixture, while black oily deposits mean it's burning oil. If it looks white and glazed, the engine is running too hot--the timing could be off. If the color is anything but light gray to light brown, make a note for your mechanic.

CHECK THE GLASS

Glass is an easy detail to overlook. Make sure you check the windows carefully for small cracks or chips that may later turn into big cracks and render its replacement. The windshield is the one most subject to nicks and chips from road pebbles. If you come across a cracked window, you'll need to call an auto glass shop for a quote. The cost of a new windshield and installation can get pretty pricey. Pay particular attention.

ABOUT SUNROOFS

I have this to say about sunroofs--know the difference between factory (original) and custom. If you're looking at a car with a factory sunroof, then you're looking at something that adds value to the car. However, a custom sunroof that some high school kid bought at the auto parts store and installed himself, or even one that was professionally installed by John Doe's Sunroofs, can actually hurt the value of a car.

Nine times out of ten custom sunroofs leak. Nine times out of ten potential used car buyers are turned off when they see a car with a custom sunroof. Most kids think they're cool, but when they pay hundreds to get one installed, not only are they out the initial cost,

CHECKING OUT THE BEAST 55

they are out hundreds more when they try to resell. Avoid cars with custom sunroofs. They're bad news.

As for factory sunroofs, whether power or manual, check the full range of movement and see that it seats properly. Check around the inside for evidence of leakage such as stained headliner or stained seats.

INTERIOR

You will also want to visually check out the interior. The front seats, the back seats, the headliner, the carpet, everything should look in order. Is the dash cracked? They are expensive to replace, so you can either live with it or do what I do and cover it up with a dash saver. They cost about 80 bucks. Put it down on your checklist.

Even though the seller told you the mileage over the phone, check it now. I've had plenty of people tell me they have 60,000 miles on their car and when I look it reads 69,900 miles. This is an easy way for people to exaggerate. What's another 9,900 miles? Keep in mind that if they exaggerate about the mileage, they'll be exaggerating about everything else. Believe what they say accordingly.

Check to see if the owner's manual is in the glove box. If it's not, ask if they have it. It's important to have the owner's manual so you can acquaint yourself with the car and learn about the maintenance schedule, oil recommendations, etc. If they don't have one, then put down $25.00 for the cost of a replacement on your checklist.

How does the driver's seat look? This will be the seat with the most wear. Is it torn or cracked? You can either live with it or do the seat-cover thing. Put it down on your checklist.

Keep in mind while you're looking at all this, everything should be in agreement with the odometer. If the car has 60,000 miles on it, then the interior should look like a car that has been driven 60,000 miles, not 160,000. If there seems to be extreme wear, like worn pedal pads on a low mileage car, then suspect odometer tampering. If the odometer doesn't run over 100,000 miles, then it could have turned over. Ask the seller. If he claims that it has not turned over, but your eyes tell you differently, then believe your eyes and assume that they are not telling the truth.

Check each of the crank-up windows and make sure they are working properly. If the car has power windows, then check each window from the master control and at each door as well. And don't be embarrassed about it. You wouldn't want to sell your car to someone without him first checking everything, would you? Make sure all doors lock and unlock manually and with the key. Ditto for power door locks.

Don't forget to check the heater in the summer and the air-conditioner in the winter. Also check the following: emergency brakes, horn, headlights (both high and low beam), turn signals, four-ways, brake lights, back-up lights, dome light, dash lights, windshield washer and wipers, and the radio. If the car is a convertible, whether it's manual or power, you'll want to check this too. Check any other power options, such as power seats, antenna, tilt steering, etc., and make notes accordingly.

Remember, if the car has something not working right, like a power window, you'll need to call the dealer to get a phone estimate for what the MAXIMUM cost would be to fix it. Make sure you do this before you make an offer to purchase. Don't disregard something that the seller may claim as trivial. You may be in shock when you find out what a new power window unit costs for a car these days.

LUGGAGE COMPARTMENT

Use the remote release to open the trunk if the car offers one. Open it with the key as well. Unless this is a truck, the spare tire is usually below the trunk matting. There should also be a jack, lug wrench, and jack handle. Is anything missing? Put it on your checklist and get prices from the dealer later. Is the spare tire a real one, or is it one of those dummy tires? I think they call them dummy tires because whoever came up with the bright idea is a big dummy.

Consider the following: You sell real estate and are enroute to a nearby town to close a six-figure deal on a house. Suddenly you have a blow out. Now, if you have a real spare, you can still make it, but if you have a dummy tire, guess what? That's right, you're hating it. You can't drive at freeway speeds safely with a dummy tire on your car. So you can forget about closing that real estate deal. Right now you have to go find a tire shop and get a new tire installed. Meanwhile, six-figure-earning decision-makers in the auto industry are busy designing their next "great" money-saving idea. The moral of the story? What's good for the auto industry isn't always good for the people.

FLOOD CARS

In times of flooding, opportunists will buy up dozens of water-damaged vehicles for next to nothing, clean them up, get them running, and ship them to another region of the country. These flood cars are to be avoided at all costs. Water will get into sealed compartments and promote rust while wreaking havoc on the car's entire electrical system via corrosion. The worst part is, the car will appear fine while these problems lie just around the corner.

The easiest way to detect a flood car is with your nose. Sniff around the interior for musty mildew. Check underneath the carpeting, floor mats, seats, and in the trunk compartment for silt and rust. Look for a water line on the interior and exterior of the car. Moisture trapped in the headlights or in the dash panel are also warning flags of a flood car. Any suspected flood car receives an automatic failure.

THE EIGHT GOLDEN RULES OF CHECKING OUT THE BEAST

1) Always show up early
2) Always look at a car in daylight
3) Always bring a flashlight
4) Know how to check for hidden body damage and rust
5) Always check inside the tail pipe
6) Arrange it so you be will checking out a cold engine
7) Thoroughly inspect the interior
8) Never be in a hurry to buy a used car

CHAPTER 4:

THE TEST DRIVE

The car has passed the body/rust inspection and doesn't seem to have a serious oil leak. You have also checked out all the previously mentioned steps and have made your notes accordingly. Now you are ready for the test drive. If you are in an unfamiliar area, you will want to have the owner direct you to a quiet side street, preferably a dead end, as well as a freeway or open road where you can cruise up to 60 mph or so.

LISTEN WITH YOUR EARS

When you do the test drive you will be listening for sounds. You will listen to the engine perform, the transmission shift, and the tires roll. What are you listening for? Anything that doesn't sound right. So, if at all possible, try to test drive the car without the owner. This way you can test drive the car without the seller right next to you babbling away about this and that and drawing your attention away from the car's performance. Most likely, though, sellers will insist on coming along, and you really can't blame them. They don't know who you are and may be worried about you not coming back at all.

60 THE USED CAR BUYER'S MANUAL

Before driving the car, start the engine with the hood still up. You want to listen to the engine. If the engine was dead cold, it should idle high, indicating that the choke is on. After a minute or two, a light tap on the accelerator should slow the engine down to normal idle speed. This should be around 800 rpms for those cars with tachometers. If the engine was already warm, the engine should idle at a low speed. Try to make a point to look at a car with a cold engine. If possible, first thing in the morning would be the optimum time.

Listen to the valves. They make a clickety-click-click-clickety-click-click sound that comes from the top of the engine. Does the clickety-click-click sound almost obnoxious, indicating loose valves? Do all the clickety-click-clicks sound equal or does one sound different from the others, indicating one loose valve?

Before you hang your head over the engine to listen, remember there are moving parts. The spinning fan blade can yank the hair right out of your head or grab your loose necktie and strangle you to death. PAY ATTENTION!

Of course, I don't expect someone with no experience to decipher what they hear, but at least you can look like you know what you're doing, which is important in front of sellers. Remember, they don't know who your are or what your background is.

Are there any other sounds that draw your attention? Do you hear a deep popping sound coming from the side or behind the engine? This could be an exhaust leak. The exhaust manifold may need some tightening down or it could be warped and in need of a new one. A new exhaust manifold is a pricey part that is difficult to replace. Your mechanic can diagnose it.

Another strange sound you may hear is an ear-piercing screech coming from the front of the engine. Sometimes it will go away once the engine is warm and sometimes it won't. The screeching usually comes from a rapidly wearing fan belt or air-conditioning belt that has its pulleys out of alignment. Cars with this problem go through a lot of belts. Again, your mechanic can diagnose it. Although it sounds like hell, it could be simple to fix and a great excuse to get the price lower.

Having test driven many cars, I have seen a lot of the same tactics. The seller talks nonstop and distracts you from your test drive. For talkative sellers, ask them nicely to be quiet so that you may listen to the engine perform. When they turn on their stereo and start bragging how they paid $1,000 for it, do what I do. Reply with, "Why don't you pull the stereo system and we'll knock $1,000 off the price?" This shuts them up really quick, every time.

CHECK THE BRAKES

You want a quiet or dead-end street to test the brakes. On a straight and level road, with no one in sight behind you, get the car up to about 30 mph. You don't want to slam on the brakes to lock them up, but you do want to hit the brakes firmly to see how well the car stops. A verbal warning to your passengers before you do this is always nice.

The pedal should feel solid without the use of extreme force. Of course, if the car has power brakes, the pedal will be much more sensitive and need less pressure. Most importantly, the car should not pull to the left or to the right. It should brake evenly. If you thought you felt a tug to one side try it again, but this time use less force and let the steering wheel slip loosely through your fingers so the car goes the direction it wants.

Of course, I don't have to remind you to be safe about this and tell you to double check for any cars in sight behind you, but I will anyway. DO IT! And be careful when you hit the brakes and let the wheel go loose. You don't want to go crashing into a parked car and have a real mess on your hands. Do this test on a road that has no traffic and allows plenty of maneuvering space.

If the car pulls to one side, straighten the car out and continue with your inspection. You have just discovered that either the brakes are out of adjustment or the car needs new brakes, period. Make a note, or, better yet, have your assistant make a note because you're still driving.

Cars that pull to one side when you brake are extremely dangerous on wet roads. If you hit the brakes hard on a wet surface, you will go into a skid. So uneven braking is something you want to get fixed pronto. Your mechanic can diagnose the problem and give you an estimate at the same time.

ABOUT BRAKE NOISES

It's a common thing for disc breaks to squeak. Sometimes they squeak when you apply the brakes and sometimes they squeak when you drive. It doesn't necessarily mean that the car needs a brake job. Most new brakes squeak until they're broken in. Just make sure you mention it to your mechanic when you bring it in. He can easily check the brake pads and discs and report to you exactly how much life is left on them.

However, there is a brake noise you should be wary of. If you apply the brakes and hear a soft grinding noise which can sometimes be felt through the brake pedal, it's a sure sign of brake pads that are spent. Not only is the car unsafe to drive, the disc rotor is being damaged every time you apply the brakes. My advice here is to turn the car around and carefully head back. The car needs new brakes immediately and you don't want to test drive it until the car is safe. If the brakes check out, continue.

CHECK THE ALIGNMENT

While still out on those straight level roads, you can test the front-end alignment. Again, do this test on a straight and level surface where there isn't any traffic. Going about 35 mph or so, let the steering wheel slip freely through your hands. If the road is straight and level, the car should go straight as well. If the car wants to go to the right or left, grab the wheel, straighten it out and try it again. Did it do it again in the same direction? It could be just uneven tire pressure, but more than likely, the car needs a front-end alignment. Remember, if it pulls to one side only when the brakes are applied then it's a brake problem.

Also, if you notice the steering wheel shimmying (vibrating abnormally) at any certain speed during the test drive, then that's a sure sign of an alignment problem. Alignment can cost anywhere from $40 to $400 depending on what may need replacing. But don't let an alignment problem stop your inspection. Make a note on your checklist and make sure you mention it to your mechanic before he inspects it. He should be able to give you an accurate estimate, which you will, of course, use for bargaining leverage.

CHECK THE TRANSMISSION

While still on one of those quiet roads, you want to check reverse. If you are in a hilly area, backing up the slope is preferred. Make sure you can see clearly behind you for a great distance. Put the car in reverse and back up slowly at first. You should have the windows down to listen for any noises. The car should back up smoothly.

If you are test driving a car with a standard transmission, step on the accelerator to increase the speed and then abruptly let off the gas. Try it again. Everything working okay? What you're trying to detect is whether the transmission pops out of reverse and into neutral (more on this shortly). If it didn't, then continue on with your inspection.

For standard transmissions, it shouldn't be difficult to find a gear, nor should it be difficult to put into a gear. The stick shift should move in and out of each gear easily. Difficulty shifting into gear is usually a sign of a worn clutch not doing its job. Unless you'd rather not hassle with getting a new clutch installed, continue with your inspection. Depending on the model, a new clutch assembly can be anywhere from $200 to $500. If your mechanic verifies that the car will need a new clutch, have him give you an estimate and use this amount as more bargaining leverage.

Stick shifters that pop out of gear while driving indicate worn teeth in the gear box which means you will need a costly overhaul or a new transmission altogether. In either case, it's an automatic failure. Steer clear of cars that pop out of gear when you drive them. Even if you could replace the transmission for $500, worn-out transmissions go hand in hand with worn-out engines. Chances are you will be needing some serious engine work soon.

For automatic tramsmissions, pay attention to how it shifts for the rest of the test drive. It should be smooth and sure, not clunky or moving in and out of speeds like it can't decide where it wants to be.

Also, whether the car is standard or automatic, any metal-to-metal grinding noises coming from the transmission should get an automatic failure from you. Drive it carefully back to the owner's house and politely leave.

THE OPEN ROAD

Next, drive the car to a freeway or open road where you can go a comfortable 60 mph. On the way to the freeway, you want to notice how the car handles around corners. It should hug the road smoothly without shimmying. Also on the way there, you are still listening for sounds and paying attention to the engine's performance. The engine and transmission should work together, accelerating and shifting smoothly, with confidence.

As you enter the freeway, don't be afraid to step on the gas, but don't be abusive either. You want to see exactly how much power this engine has to offer and how well the transmission shifts from one gear to the next. When you get up to 50 mph or so, keep it steady for a moment. If the road isn't crowded, try the alignment test again. Does it hold true or does it pull to the right or left?

At 50 mph, imagine you are following a slowpoke on a two-lane highway and you need to pass him quickly. With no one if front of you, step down on the gas to see what kind of passing power the engine has. Is the engine very responsive or does it lag for a moment before kicking in? A responsive engine is what we like to see, but a hesitation at 50 mph usually means one of three things: Either there's a problem with carburetion/injection, or a problem with the automatic transmission taking too long to shift into the right gear (standard drivers--make sure you are in the right gear), or that's just the way the car is and you have to live with it. Most of the time it's the latter case. Make sure you remember to make a note on your checklist to mention this to your mechanic later.

When you return from your test drive, check again with your flashlight under the hood and under the car for anything leaking. Most fluid leaks become more severe once the engine is hot.

ABOUT RECEIPTS

Don't be shy about asking for them. If someone claims they have kept all their receipts and informs you that a new clutch was installed last month, don't believe them until you verify the receipt yourself. PEOPLE WILL LIE ABOUT WORK DONE TO THEIR CAR! They have a good motive. They're trying to sell you a car.

Plenty of times I have called on a receipt that sellers have claimed possession of and they were unable to produce it. Somehow the one from last month's clutch job mysteriously disappeared! When this happens, their claim of repair loses validity. These people are playing with you. People who save all their receipts don't lose the big ones from last month.

When you do look at a receipt, make sure it belongs to the car that the owner claims. Check the date, year, make, and model, and somewhere on there will be the license plate number. Also, the mileage of the car at the time of repair should be logged in there as well. All this information should coincide with what the seller is saying about his car.

Pay particular attention to the mileage. This is where you can catch evidence of odometer tampering. Is the amount currently on the car more than what was logged on the receipt in the past? Keep in mind that many vehicle odometers won't go over 100,000 miles, which means they will turn over and start again. So if the owner claims that the 58,000 miles currently on the odometer is the actual mileage and you notice 95,000 miles on a three-year-old receipt, you know the odometer has either been tampered with or the car has 158,000 miles on it. Watch out for this.

THE CHARACTER THING

How do you drive your car? Do you drive it hard (quick accelerations and heavy braking) or do you generally take it easy? Do you change the oil every 3,000 miles or whenever you get around to it? Do you wash and clean your car regularly or do you tend to let it go? Do you have the major services performed on schedule as the owner's manual states, or do you stretch as far as you can?

This is all part of the character thing. You know how you treat your car, and when looking at a used auto you need to try to figure out what kind of person the seller is and how he treated his car. Was he the kind who took it easy or drove it hard? Is he retired or is he eighteen years old? Is his house and yard neat in appearance or does it have kids toys strewn about and peeling paint on the house?

So remember, the whole time you're checking out a used car you're also checking out the seller. What kind of person is he or she? You need to make a character judgement in twenty minutes. Find out about this person through observation and small talk. You can get a feel for what kind of driver he is and how well he cared for his car.

People take care of their cars the same way they take care of their houses and yards. It may sound silly, but it's true. I want to tell you a story, and I'll keep it short. Being the camper and outdoor enthusiast that I am, I decided I was going to buy a camper. I found one advertised that was just around the corner, so I went over to have a look. While I was knocking on the solid oak front door, I noticed badly peeling varnish. I mean, it looked horrible and stood out like a sore thumb.

A middle-aged gentleman opened the door and invited me in. His camper was in the backyard, and he would lead me through his house to get there. As soon as I stepped inside there was a staircase that went up to the left. On every step there were boxes and stuff stacked up to where there was just barely enough room to pass by. The first thing that entered my mind was that they must be in the middle of moving.

Stepping over kids' toys on the way to the living room, we passed the open kitchen area. Every counter top was covered with magazines, newspapers and Lord knows what else. Through the living room you had to watch your step for more kids' toys and junk that lined the floor. The areas of carpeting that were exposed looked so matted, I figured it hadn't been vacuumed in years.

Through a dirty sliding glass door and by a filthy pool surrounded by broken pool toys was where he had his camper set up.

"It's just been sitting here for two years as the kids' play room," he said as the knot in my stomach tightened. I poked my nose inside and saw things broken and missing, and junk all over the place. The camper was so filthy dirty inside and out, I was disgusted. And it takes a lot to disgust me. I used my "just-started-looking" excuse and high-tailed it out of there.

With that said, it's easy to see the relation here. Sometimes it's not that obvious, and you need to look a little closer to find those telltale signs that reveal the type of character you're dealing with. If you're buying a car from an owner whose house and yard is neat and tidy, you have reason to feel good about the car. You are buying from an owner who takes pride in ownership.

However, if the seller's garage and yard look like a war zone, you have reason to be uneasy even if his auto checks out by your mechanic. You'll never know what sins have been committed until later. The moral of the story? It pays to be observant.

A WASTE OF TIME AND MONEY?

Some of you may think that going to a mechanic is a waste of your time and money, especially if you just thoroughly checked out the car yourself. On the other hand, some of you may wonder why bother with checking it over yourself when you can have a mechanic do it more competently. I would like to answer both of these up front.

First of all, not even a mechanic knows for sure what condition an engine is in until he has compression tested it and test driven it. You could buy a car that seems to be running well, but it may really need a valve job or it could have a cylinder with a broken ring or it may need the top-end completely rebuilt. In any case, it will cost you plenty to get it corrected. So if you spend 50 bucks and have a mechanic report this, don't think of it as 50 dollars down the drain.

You just saved yourself a lot of money and headaches. This is money well spent.

As far as not inspecting the car yourself and relying totally on the mechanic, you'll be paying out a lot of money in mechanic's fees when cars fail inspection on simple things you could have caught yourself.

This is why you should learn how to thoroughly inspect a car. You're weeding out the undesirables and bringing only the ones that passed your rigorous inspection to the mechanic. And once the car has passed his inspection, you'll own a car that will allow you to sleep peacefully at night.

GOING TO YOUR MECHANIC

Now that you have found a car that has passed every test and inspection listed above, the next step is to have it inspected by your mechanic. Tell the seller you are interested in buying the car, but first wish to have it looked at by your mechanic at your own expense. Most people won't object to this, especially when they know their car is in fine shape.

If, for any reason, the seller won't allow you to do this, tell him you're sorry you couldn't do business and walk away. Don't let him make up excuses why he can't get the time to do it. If he wants to sell his car, he will have to make time. Having a car checked over is a common practice, so don't let him talk you out of it. Either he lets you have your mechanic check it out or the deal's off--period.

Why do I feel strongly about this? Because there are plenty of people selling used cars with hidden defects who will tell you otherwise... "Ah you don't need no mechanic to look at this, it runs perfect. Besides, I'm very busy with my work and don't have time and da da-da da-da..." No matter how sincere, trust no one.

People who do this usually have something to hide. If something is wrong with his car, he knows your mechanic will catch it, thus keeping him from selling it to you. So be especially wary of anyone trying to talk you out of seeing your mechanic. Either he succumbs to your request or you walk. It's that simple.

Most of the time, people won't mind having their cars inspected. What you need to do is call your mechanic as soon as possible to schedule an appointment when it's convenient for the seller to meet you at your mechanic's shop. Your mechanic should spend a good hour checking things out. This is the time to give him that list of notes you made about things in question, such as brake noises, oil seepage, etc.

He should do a compression test, battery and charging test, frame inspection, fluid leakage inspection, alignment and suspension check, brake inspection, and test drive the car for engine and transmission performance. When it's all said and done, he should report to you in private about his findings.

In most cases, the car will have several less serious things wrong that will start adding up. He will tell you about the current problems as well as the problems that are just around the corner. It may need front brakes soon and tires all the way around, etc. Your mechanic can give you accurate estimates on repairs; and from his report you can make any necessary adjustments to your proposed offer.

Your mechanic may ask you what the selling price is and advise you on what to offer. This may be good advice but, remember, that's his opinion. Don't let this keep you from making an offer lower than what the mechanic thinks is a fair price. Even though what you had in mind may seem like a low-pitch offer, you can back it up with the mechanic's report, which gives you muscle to bargain with.

In other words, you're not someone B.S.'ing the sellers about something you think may be wrong. You have it in writing by a certified mechanic which the sellers can see for themselves. When they find problems with their car that they didn't know about before, they usually become more flexible in their price. Who knows, they may even succumb to your first offer, which would recoup that $50 mechanic's bill many times over.

Remember, if your mechanic tells you right off the bat there's something seriously wrong and advises you that the car is a bad buy, don't get frustrated thinking you just threw away 50 bucks. In actuality, you saved hundreds or maybe even thousands by dodging a car with a serious problem. In addition, you just gained some valuable experience that can be applied when looking at your next car.

DOUBLE CHECK FOR RECALLS

Between the time you find a car and the time you hand over the cash, you should check to see if the car has had any recalls and, if so, whether they were corrected. A good time to do this would be when you are waiting for your mechanic to complete his inspection.

This can be easily done with one phone call to the respective dealership for the car you're considering. You will need the Vehicle's Indentification Number, so copy it down before you call. Within a matter of minutes, the service department will give you the status of that specific car. You will know immediately whether or not the car has a recall that needs to be addressed.

Even though recall problems are repaired free by the manufacturer, there is the inconvenience of having to take time out of your busy day to get it corrected. This could be used as another excuse to lower the price a little more. Consider using it for additional bargaining leverage.

THE SIX GOLDEN RULES OF THE TEST DRIVE

1) Listen for anything that doesn't sound right
2) Ask for, and check, all receipts
3) Observe the owner's characteristics
4) Take the car to your mechanic
5) Check the recall history
6) Never be in a hurry to buy a used car

CHAPTER 5:

NEGOTIATING

Haggling can be the thrill of the kill for some and the agony of the purchase for others. Wherever you place yourself in the spectrum, remember this: Smart negotiating can save you hundreds of dollars right off the bat. There's nothing to be bashful about or ashamed of. It's your hard-earned money. Make the seller earn it.

If you are one of those who is not comfortable with negotiating, keep in mind that the people with whom you are dealing with may not be comfortable with it either. By playing tough, you can capitalize on their fear of haggling and create an edge for yourself without even trying hard.

Negotiating with a private party will occur in three phases. In the first phase, you will prenegotiate or precondition the seller to lower his price.

In the second phase, you will negotiate with the seller and agree upon a price with the assumption that your mechanic does not find anything wrong. If, however, your mechanic does find a problem(s) that you missed, this will open the door for further negotiations.

The final phase, obviously, is renegotiating after your mechanic has looked the car over and caught a few minor things that you were not aware of. You add up the total estimate for repairs and approach the seller with your new offer based on the additional findings.

PHASE 1: PRECONDITIONING

The preconditioning phase begins with the phone call when you ask, "How much are you asking for it?" You will ask this same question at least two more times: once during the visual inspection and once during or immediately following the test drive.

When calling on an ad, even if the price is stated clearly in bold letters, ask the question anyway. This works best after a question you had just asked drew a negative response about the car. For example, if you ask, "How many miles are on it?" and their answer reveals high mileage, or you ask, "What shape is the body in?" and their answer reveals a scratch on the hood, this would be the perfect time to ask "How much are you asking for it?"

This preconditions sellers to lower their price, which they may do immediately over the phone. When sellers compensate you over the phone for a fault with their car, they set the stage for further deductions for any additional faults you may find during your inspection. If they don't lower the price over the phone, then they should let you know in their answer that they will compensate you for their car's faults. They will most likely tell you right out that their price is negotiable or that they are accepting offers, etc.

During your visual inspection, touch every little flaw on the car, making sure the seller sees you. Then go back and touch the biggest visual flaw the car has and ask again, "How much are you asking for this car?" as if you couldn't believe they wanted so much. The seller may lower his price again just to keep you interested. Even if it's only a little, it puts you that much closer to making a deal.

For the test drive segment, again, find another major flaw related to the mechanics of the car. Is the car out of alignment and pulling to one side? Does the car need a new muffler? Mention the problem(s) to the seller.

To keep from sounding like a broken record when you ask the third time, say, "I'm sorry, but I've called on so many cars this past week; how much did you say you were asking for this car?" Boom. You have just informed the seller that you are a serious buyer who is not afraid to shop around. He knows that, if he is to sell his car, he better lower his price a little more.

Another form of preconditioning works when you have called and left a message on a seller's recorder. Let's say the car you called on was an '89 model advertised in the classifieds for $3,500. When he calls back you deliberately say "I'm sorry, but I have called on a bunch of cars today. Was yours the '89 selling for $3,000?" Now the seller believes there is another car on the market, the same year as his, selling for $500 less. He realizes he will have to bargain if he wants to sell you his car. He may respond with, "No, mine was for $3,500, but the price is negotiable." Bingo! This translates to "No, mine was for $3,500, but I'd probably take $3,000 for it." You just got $500 dollars knocked off the price without even looking at the car yet. That's a sizeable reduction. Preconditioning really works. Try it.

PHASE 2: NEGOTIATING BEFORE THE MECHANIC'S INSPECTION

Preconditioning is a way to get the seller to lower the price or prepare him to lower the price before you make your offer. At the beginning of the second negotiation phase you want to continue with this momentum of getting the seller to come down as low as possible. This will create an edge for you by cutting the spread between his asking price and your target purchase price without you having yet made an offer.

As for deciding on your target purchase price, that's something you consider only after inspecting and test driving the car. You must decide what would be the most you'd be willing to fork over for this particular car (with the assumption that your mechanic doesn't find any significant flaws, of course) and do your best to get the seller to meet you there. When you reach the final phase of negotiation, you may need to readjust your target purchase price when the mechanic informs you of problems that you were unaware of.

Before submitting your offer, don't get too greedy and attempt to suck the seller bone dry by making an offer way below the asking price, especially if he didn't seem too receptive during preconditioning. Save the bone-sucking for the final phase. Besides, at this point he may take it as an insult and tell you to take a walk.

So how do you know where to start with your first offer? Judging by the responses you received during the preconditioning phase, you should have a good idea of how open the seller is to a low-pitch offer. Did he appear rigid or receptive to lower offers? Before you submit any offer, there are still more things to consider:

• **The condition and price of the car** - Is the car in near perfect condition and priced at fair market value, or is there a dent in the fender and the price seems high? If the car is in excellent shape and priced fairly, then be more conservative in your offer. But when a car has several minor problems and seems overpriced, by all means, make that low offer.

- **Feel the seller out** - Ask why he is selling the car and if anyone else has looked at it yet. Even though you asked the same questions over the phone, ask him again to see if the answers vary. Is he moving or in need of money for other reasons? Has no one else looked at it, and his phone hasn't been ringing? Do you detect a bit of desperation in his voice? If this is the case, don't hesitate to make that low pitch offer.

- **The car's immediate needs** - Does the car need immediate repair work, i.e., brakes, tires, paint, etc., that the seller told you about or that you discovered on your own? The more immediate needs the car has, the more liberal you can be with your low offer.

After carefully weighing all these considerations, tell the seller you are interested in buying the car (that is, if you still are), but have a problem with the price. Ask what his bottom price is and see what kind of response you get. Whatever price he comes up with, don't accept it as written in stone. Chances are he will go lower, but is just testing the negotiation waters with you.

Okay, enough of all this jibber-jabber. It's example time. Let's say you were looking at a car that was advertised for $5,900. After inspecting and test driving the car, the most you'd be willing to pay is an even $5,000. You came to this conclusion because the mileage is a little high, it will be needing new tires soon, and the past months of studying the market tells you the asking price of $5,900 is inflated.

During the preconditioning phase, the seller knocks off $300 for the flaws you point out, which puts you $600 away from your target price. You tell the seller you are very interested, but have a problem with the price. You then press him for his bottom price and he says he couldn't let it go for anything less than $5,300. With your target price of $5,000 in mind, you would want to offer $4,800, which gives you $200 in bargaining leeway to come up to your price.

Your offer, by the way, is made with the understanding that your mechanic won't find any problems. If he does, then you will be allowed to renegotiate a new sale price for the car. It's always wise to make this crystal clear to the seller before you take the car to your mechanic. This will prevent any misunderstandings when you begin renegotiating and is also another great way to precondition the seller for the possibility of a lower price.

The seller says no to $4,800 and sticks to his $5,300 offer. You then remind him of all that is wrong with the car and the fact that you have several other cars on your list you have yet to look at. Tell him you really want to make this work between you, but he will have to do better than that. The seller goes another $50, making it $5,250. You counter offer $4,850, matching his $50. You are now $400 apart and $250 from your target price.

This would be a good time to change the subject and compliment the seller in some way about his car, home, child, etc. Talk a little bit and ease the tension between you. Some good buttering up can help melt his price some more. Tell the seller how well he cared for his car and how you appreciate people like him who take care of their things. Tell him how you are the same way with your own vehicles and that his car will be well cared for if you were to buy it. Some people get attached to their cars, like pets, and would rather see them go to a good home. Hey, it never hurts to try.

Getting back on the negotiation track, tell him that although the car isn't your favorite color, you are ready to leave a deposit if you can just agree on a price. Remind him how the final payment will be all cash. Coax him. "$4,850. What do you say?" The seller finally budges to $5,200. You then go for broke with your take-it-or-leave-it offer. You tell him this is it; your budget only allowed for $4,800, but you can borrow the rest from a friend to pay an even $5,000 for his car. Be firm. Tell him that's it, take it or leave it. The seller hesitates, scratches his head, hems and haws, and then tries to get you to split the difference and meet at $5,100. You stand firm and say no.

Now, at this point, a hundred dollars above your target price is pretty darn good and if the seller doesn't go for it, you should consider taking it for $5,100. Remember, you will have another chance to get this price lower after your mechanic's inspection. But for the sake of negotiation, and saving money, you are ready to challenge his offer just to see if he really is at his bottom.

If, after further coaxing, the seller still refuses to accept $5,000, ask him if he's sure and remind him of the three other cars on your list you have yet to look at. Don't be afraid to walk away to call his bluff. If he doesn't give in to $5,000, you can always turn around and reconsider, taking the car for $5,100. Chances are, though, he won't let you go and will succumb to your offer. Now the car is yours for $5,000 and you still have an opportunity to get it for a lower price when your mechanic finds a few things wrong that you missed.

A deposit of $100 should be sufficient to have the seller take the car off the market for the day or two you need to get it to your mechanic. Make sure you get a receipt that states that the deposit is refundable should the deal fall through. If the seller will allow it, write a check for the deposit with the mention that the balance will be paid in cash. This way, if the deal falls through and the seller tries to pull a shenanigan, your check is proof of your deposit and you can put a stop-payment on the check if neccessary.

PHASE 3: NEGOTIATING AFTER THE MECHANIC'S INSPECTION

Now, considering it takes a day or two to get an appointment with your mechanic, time has passed since you negotiated to $5,000 with the seller. By now the seller has gotten comfortable with selling his car for $5,000 and is probably excited about getting paid and moving on with his life. When the seller meets you at your mechanic's shop motivated to sell his car, the odds are in your favor of getting his price down a little more.

After the mechanic has inspected the car and consulted privately with you on some new faults that will need attention, have him write up an estimate for everything that needs to be done. For our example's sake, let's say your mechanic found that the car is due for a front brake job, and both axle boots are torn and in need of replacement. His estimate for the work is $250, not including tax.

Approach the seller with your mechanic's report in hand and let him read the bad news. Be gentle, but firm, and give him an option. Either he pays to have the repairs corrected or you deduct the amount from the $5,000 and take the car right now for $4,750. If the seller objects, claiming that he has already come down enough to absorb that, remind him that the price you had agreed on before was under the assumption that there wasn't anything else wrong with the car. Now you have a report that shows axle boots and brake work is needed. In most cases, the seller will give in, but not always.

If the seller happens to be the home mechanic type and claims he can do it himself or has a friend that will do it cheap, tell him that's fine, but once that the car has been repaired you will want to bring it back to your mechanic to make sure the repairs were indeed performed and performed correctly (your mechanic should inspect the questioned repairs for free).

If the seller does not have this option, he would be smart to take your offer of $4,750 rather than having the repairs done by his or your mechanic. Not only will he still get paid today, he won't have the hassle of having to make an appointment and waiting days until the car is ready to sell. Plus, it's not uncommon for unforeseen problems to crop up during repairs which can inflate the estimate significantly. Also, tax wasn't included in the $250 estimate. Mention all this to him and get him thinking how he should take the money and run.

If the seller doesn't want to do either, because he feels he has already come down enough to absorb these additional costs, bargain with him on the $250 estimate. If he isn't willing to knock off the $250, what would he be willing to take off the price in order to save the deal?

Remind the seller about the brake job that needs to be done and two axle boots which are in need of replacement, neither of which you knew about before. Had you known, you would have never agreed on the $5,000 price tag. If the seller still doesn't want to budge, pick the most expensive of the two repairs and tell him that if he compensates you for the cost of that one repair, you will pay for the rest on your own. This will usually get him to act.

However, if he still won't move, don't be afraid to challenge him again. He may be bluffing. Be prepared to shake his hand and tell him how sorry you are you couldn't make this work. After getting your deposit refunded, go back into your mechanic's office and chew the fat with him a minute or two to give the seller some time to change his mind, then walk slowly for your car. If the seller hasn't approached you by the time you have gotten inside your car and put the key in the ignition, then he really is at his bottom.

Now you have to decide if you want to pay $5,000 plus the $250 in repairs (and possibly more) for this car or keep looking. If $5,250 is still well within your budget, you may want to reconsider and grab the seller before he leaves. If, however, your budget is tight and there are more cars on your list to check out, keep looking.

The above example is just that, an example. Every situation is different. If the seller was firm in his price you probably won't get too far in the first or second phase of negotiations. Phase three is where you'll likely gain some ground with a mechanic's report revealing problems in need of attention. If the seller was unaware of these problems, he will likely compensate you. The most important thing to remember is to exercise your negotiation power through each of the three steps and, in the end, you will come out the winner.

EMOTION CONTROL

Buying a used car can get very emotional and it's extremely important to hide your emotions when negotiating. This isn't always easy to do. Consider the following: You've looked at six cars in the past month. Three were junk and two others you had checked out by your mechanic failed because of hidden body damage. With the last car you called about you were certain you had finally found your car, but someone else swooped in and bought it before you even had a chance to look at it.

At this point, you are down a $100 in mechanic's fees, your frustration level is high, and your patience is worn thin. You need to find a car. Finally, you come across the perfect car. It has all the right features, it runs excellent and checks out with your mechanic, and it's even your favorite color. You are happy as a lark.

Do you know what happens when the seller sees your face beaming while you're doing cartwheels of joy? Suddenly he gets real firm in his price. He knows he has a buyer who wants his car bad, and is unlikely to budge in price. If you want to get anywhere with the seller at the negotiation table, then your emotions have to be 180 degrees from this. You have to be deadpan.

Remember, the seller will be observing you as well. When you're checking out the car you must act like you're not impressed with it. Even though inside you're screaming with joy, on the surface you must convince the seller that you're not really interested that much. This keeps the seller guessing as to whether you will even make an offer and he will remain much more flexible when it is time to haggle. It's the reverse-psychology thing. Think like a poker player who's just been dealt an ace-high full-house. You wouldn't want to give yourself away, would you?

Plenty of times I have looked at cars that were reasonably priced where I would have gladly paid the full amount, but instead I bought them for hundreds less. Even though I was willing to pay what they were asking, I would still make a lower offer. If they say no then I make another offer closer to their price. What's the worst that could happen? They don't budge, and you pay full price. But nine times out of ten they will bend a little, if not a lot. And when they do, you have recouped that money spent on mechanic's fees, giving you even more reason to be happy as a lark.

OTHER NEGOTIATION TIPS

Earlier I had mentioned briefly about prices that are followed by the word "firm." This means that the seller doesn't want to budge in price. However, DON'T LET IT KEEP YOU FROM TRYING. For some people, "firm" simply means they want to get close to their asking price. This could be a couple of hundred dollars less.

Again, every situation is different. Feel the person out. Has the car been for sale very long? Has anyone looked at it before you? The seller may realize the price is too high from the lack of interest in it. You'd be surprised how many times I bought "firm" cars for hundreds less! As in all types of negotiating, you never know until you ask.

Throughout the three phases of bargaining, whenever the seller comes back with a new offer, make some immediate gesture indicating that it's unacceptable. Grunt, moan, raise your eyebrows, flinch, scream, do something to show that the offer they just made is still out of the ball park. If you don't show some sign of dismay, the seller will think the offer he just made is within reason, since you didn't seem bothered by it.

When making your first offer, always give yourself bargaining room to come up to your target purchase price. If the asking price is $4,500 and you only want to pay $4,000, then offer $3,500. If you offer $4,000, the seller will counter-offer, expecting you to come up in price to meet him. In this case, it would probably be at $4,250, which is $250 more than you wanted to pay.

Why not offer the $4,000 as a take-it-or-leave-it offer? Because, first of all, if the person you're dealing with is any kind of a negotiator, he will expect you to come up a little more in price regardless of you saying take it or leave it. Second, if the person you're dealing with isn't too hip on negotiating, he may let it go for even lower than $4,000.

Another important tip in negotiating is assuming what the seller's target price is. When you don't see the word "firm" in the ad, always count on the seller padding the price to allow some negotiating room. Although it's no guarantee, most cars advertised at $2,200, $2,300, $2,400, or $2,500 will likely have a $2,000 seller's target price, while cars listed at $3,200, $3,300, $3,400, and $3,500 will likely have a $3,000 seller's target price, so on and so forth. As a general rule of thumb, always count on $200 to $500 added to a seller's target price. When reading the ads, you can use this information to stay within your budget.

And one last note. You can apply these negotiation techniques when you go to purchase a house or a business and save yourself thousands. Should you need some work done to your property and a contractor presents you with a bid, that bid is also open to negotiation. Should you ever find yourself as a purchaser in a corporate environment, shrewd negotiating can save the company hundreds of thousands and earn promotions. So learning this art by practicing on used cars can certainly lead to much bigger savings later in life.

TRANSFER OF VEHICLE OWNERSHIP

Because all states vary, you will need to contact your motor vehicle department ahead of time to find out exactly what is required when a change of ownership occurs. Currently in California, you need a signed Certificate of Title, also known as a pink slip, a Release of Liability sent in by the seller, a Smog Certificate, and an Odometer Disclosure Statement.

Before you hand over any cash, the seller should have in possession a Certificate of Title which proves he is the owner of the vehicle that he is selling. On the title should be the Vehicle Identification Number (VIN), license plate number, year, make, and model of the car. The VIN should match that on the car. Check these numbers BEFORE you buy the car, not after.

Starting with all 1969 models, you will find the VIN on the dash under the windshield on the driver's side, which is read from outside through the glass. Most newer autos will also have the VIN stamped on a plate that is mounted on the firewall under the hood. On some sports cars and imports you may find the VIN on the driver's side door jam as well. Prior to 1969, the placement of the VIN was random. Look for a stamped plate around the engine compartment area or in the door jams.

If you can't find a stamped plate with the VIN anywhere, if there seems to be some tampering, or if the seller has lost the title to their car, quietly leave. I recommend that you call your state police department with the car's license plate number in hand. Ask them to check it out for you. You wouldn't want to buy a stolen car, would you?

The seller's signature on the title releases his interest. If there is a lienholder on the title, such as a bank, then the lienholder needs to sign to release his interest as well. Do not hand over any cash until the lienholder has signed; otherwise, you will be assuming what is still owed on the car.

In California, the seller should have you fill out a Release of Liability. This protects him in case you should have an accident or receive a parking ticket before you get the chance to register the car in your name. It is the seller's responsibility to have this filled out and sent in, not the buyer's.

Starting with all 1966 models registered in California, a smog certificate is required every time a vehicle changes hands. According to the DMV (Department of Motor Vehicles), it should be taken care of by the seller; however, the seller can negotiate this with the buyer, making it the buyer's responsibility. If this is the case, get the seller to compensate you for the cost in the sales price.

So, Californians, when shopping around for your mechanic it is important to find one who does smog inspections, or at least knows what to look for in the area of smog equipment. You don't want to end up with a car that has smog equipment missing. It could cost you a bundle to replace. YOU WON'T BE ALLOWED TO REGISTER THE VEHICLE UNTIL IT PASSES SMOG!

The Odometer Disclosure Statement is a new form required by the DMV only for vehicles with the old style of title. Since you won't know in advance which title the seller will have, pick up a form at your nearby DMV and have the seller fill this out reqardless. It's a simple form to complete where the seller confirms whether the mileage on the odometer is actual or not. Should a seller lie about this, he could get a big fat fine and possibly a jail term to boot.

Another requirement in California is a Bill of Sale when the seller's name isn't the same name as that on the title. It is a good policy, however, to make out a bill of sale for your own records, regardless. If you don't have an official Bill of Sale form, you can easily hand-write one. Just make sure you put down the year, make, model, VIN, and plate number along with your name, the seller's name, and the agreed-upon price. You don't need anything fancy, just a sentence or two describing how you are buying such-and-such vehicle from so-and-so for X number of dollars on this date, etc. Make sure the seller signs and dates it.

Although the current registration certificate isn't required for transfer of ownership in California, you want to be aware of vehicles with out-dated registrations. Unless a current non-operational status has been filed with the state, a car with an out-dated registration translates to stiff penalties for the next victim who registers it. These could amount to hundreds of dollars. So if you're looking at a car that hasn't been registered in a few years, you better find out from your motor vehicle department how much is owed in back registration penalties before you purchase or you could get stung.

SALVAGE TITLES

A salvage title can mean several things, all of which are bad. The car may have been stolen, stripped, and recovered; it could have been in a major accident; or worse yet, it could have been damaged in a flood. In any case, when the insurance company finds the car is not worth repairing, the a car receives a salvage title from the DMV before getting auctioned off to a junk dealer, repair shop, or body man who will make the repairs with the intention of selling the patched-up car for a profit.

The "Salvage" stamp on the title remains there for the life of the car. To no surprise, the car sells for much less than cars with a clean title. To be on the safe side, any car with a salvage title should get an automatic failure from you.

THE SEVEN GOLDEN RULES OF NEGOTIATION

1) Control your emotions - no gloating when you find a car you adore
2) Precondition, precondition, precondition
3) Negotiate to the lowest possible price before going to your mechanic
4) Negotiate to the lowest possible price after the car has been inspected
5) If negotiation doesn't go your way, always remain polite and professional
6) Check over the title and registration documents thoroughly
7) Don't buy a salvage title car
8) Never be in a hurry to buy a used car

PART II:

HOW TO SELL YOUR USED CAR

CHAPTER 6:

SELLING YOUR USED CAR

This book wouldn't be complete if I didn't include a chapter on how to sell your car. In the following chapter I offer some great advice designed to help you sell your car quickly, and for its maximum worth. Even if you don't have a car to sell you should consider reading this chapter because it will put you in the seller's shoes and give you a different point of view.

Why are you selling your car? That's the most important thing to ask when you call about a car and, undoubtedly, will be asked of you when you go to sell yours. So you better be prepared.

Why *are* you selling your car? If you are selling your car because it's a lemon, I'm not for burning people. That's not what this book is about. Even though you got burned on the deal, tighten up your belt one more notch and accept the loss. Sell your lemon for whatever it's worth and chock it up to experience. And, by the way, you probably wouldn't want to sell it to a friend or an acquaintance. If the car was a problem for you, it will be a problem for them, so you won't be winning any popularity contests from whoever buys it.

Let's consider the real reasons people sell their cars:

Reason #1: It's a lemon. It was nothing but a problem from day one. Or it's an orange. There were some problems with the car and it wasn't all that bad, but they wouldn't buy another one.
Reason #2: They're tired of it. They've had it five years now and are ready for a change.
Reason #3: They're upgrading/downgrading. "We're buying a brand new car." "My wife is pregnant and we need a 4-door sedan now." "I need to get a truck for my business." "All our kids have moved out, and I always wanted a sports car."
Reason #4: They're moving out of state, overseas, to another planet, etc.
Reason #5: They need money. "My wife is pregnant, and I have to sell my convertible." "We owe Uncle Sam big time this year."
Reason #6: They don't need/drive it anymore. "It was an extra car that has been sitting for a long time."

Reasons #3 through #6 are the ones I like to hear when I call about a car. Reason #2 can be okay, but whenever I hear it I become very wary that there's a hidden problem with the car. It's the most common reason people use when in fact the real reason is Reason #1. Of course, you won't ever hear anyone use Reason #1 and neither should you, unless you don't want to sell it. Whether you have a real lemon or just an orange on your hands, use Reason #2. After all, you're telling the truth. You *are* tired of it.

If your auto has had countless repairs, it's up to you to decide if you should offer that information to a potential buyer. One thing to consider, though; a car with countless repairs when there's only 60 or 80 thousand miles on it will look bad in the eyes of the buyer. They will think that the car hasn't been cared for properly or that it is problematic. You may just want to offer information on the big things that have been done, such as a new transmission, new clutch, new engine, etc. These may seem attractive to the buyer. They will think the car has a new life. And hopefully you saved your receipts and can back up what you say.

PREPPING YOUR CAR FOR SALE

Nothing can help sell a car quicker than a nice detail job. People get turned off real fast when they see a dirty car with a filthy interior and

SELLING YOUR USED CAR 87

grimy engine compartment. Whether you're the kind of person who keeps his or her car spotless, or tends to let things go, now is the time to make that set of wheels sparkle. Is your engine running rough and in need of a tune-up? If it is, get it taken care of now. Tune-ups aren't that expensive.

The next step would be to fix all the little things you have been putting off that are inexpensive to replace. Broken window cranks, missing door lock knobs, frayed wiper blades, etc., things like these are nickle-and-dime stuff that can be easily replaced. You want to eliminate all the negatives on you car. In the case of something that costs a few bucks, like a broken tail-light lens, try calling around to the salvage yards. If you have a common car, chances are good that you will find the part you need and save yourself some dough by avoiding the cost of new.

Is your car running fine and all the little things have been fixed? If it is, then you are ready to start detailing. There are two ways you can go about this. You can pay someone else to do it or you can do it yourself.

THE LAZY PERSON'S WAY

If you have some extra money that you don't mind parting with, you could drop your car off at an auto detailing shop for a few hours. There they will steam clean your engine, wash and wax your car, and clean your upholstery and carpets all for about a $100, give or take. If your car's paint is faded from the sun, the auto detailer will buff out the paint with a polishing compound which will do wonders for your car's look. It's well worth the extra charge.

THE PERSON-WITH-A-LOT-OF-ENERGY WAY

If you're into saving money and have some extra time (and energy), you could easily do it yourself. You will want to arm yourself with some good cleaners for the vinyl, upholstery, and tires. As for the greasy engine compartment, take it to a detail shop just for the engine steam clean. You should be able to get this service for $25 or so and then you can do the rest of the cleaning yourself. The engine wash should be the first step in cleaning your car.

Give your car a good hand wash, including under the wheel wells and door jams. If your car has spent a lot of time in the sun, its paint will be faded. Get yourself some polishing compound and follow the directions. You'll want to rub it out before waxing it. And by the way, buffing out your car with polishing compound requires some elbow grease. You'll get a sore hand, but it's worth it in the end.

After washing and buffing out your car you'll want to wax it with a good brand of wax. And with your hand already sore from buffing it out, this would be a good time to recruit an assistant.

For tires, there are cleaners on the market now where you just spray it on and let it drip off. It doesn't get much easier than that. How are your rims/wheel covers? You'll want them to match the rest of the car, so get the appropriate cleaner and take care of them too.

For the interior, get out the vacuum cleaner and upholstery cleaner and window cleaner and go to it. A scrub brush will help you get any stains out of the seats. For dust in hard-to-get places like inside the air vents, use Q-tips. Don't forget the trunk and spare tire compartment. Clean! Clean! Clean! Once you have finished, your car will look so good you may decide not to sell it after all!

CALIFORNIA RESIDENTS ONLY

If you live in California, the Department of Motor Vehicles designates the seller as the responsible party for getting the car smogged. As I mentioned before, you can always negotiate this with the buyer if you really don't want to hassle with it. But keep in mind, you'll find that people will try to knock $50 or $100 off your asking price just for smog, even though it costs less than $30 for the inspection and certificate. Their alibi is there could be some adjustments or something in need of repair in order to get it to pass smog, which will cost more money.

Do yourself a favor; if you know that your car will pass smog with no problem, do it. The certificate is good for 90 days, which is more than enough time to sell your car. This way the buyer will have one less area to haggle with you when you show him the certificate.

ASKING PRICE

As described in the **Research** chapter of this book, you will be constantly scanning the ads to see what the market is getting for the type of car(s) you're after. So as long as you're already reading the ads, watch to see how much cars identical to yours are going for as well. This is the most accurate information you have that will tell what your car is worth.

Also in the **Research** chapter, you were to find out what the book price is of the car you are researching. As long as you're at it, find out what your own car is listed for. If your car is in primo condition with low miles then you should add to the price, just as the book states. But if your car has something major wrong with it, like a big dent, obviously it won't be worth as much as the price guide states. The general rule of thumb, however, when figuring how much to advertise your car for, is that it's always wise to start high. You can always come down, but you can't go back up.

As I described before, you want to pad your asking price in anticipation of negotiating. Always pad your price by about 20 percent for cars under $3,000; i.e., if you want $1,000 for your car, ask $1,200. If you want $2,000 for your car, ask $2,400, etc. For cars that you expect to sell for $3,000 or more, don't pad your price by more than $500 or you will get too far out of the market range and throw money away on ads.

ADVERTISING

Your car is running its best, it's all detailed and looking good, and you California residents had it smogged. You are ready to run your first ad. As I mentioned earlier in this book, there are plenty of places to advertise your car, so how do you decide which publication to start in? If there are any publications in your area that offer free classified advertising, like we have here in Southern California, then by all means take advantage. Unless there's some kind of emergency in your life and you are in a big hurry to sell, there's no need to grand slam every venue with an ad. This will guarantee you a big advertising bill when maybe only one ad would have worked fine.

Remember I said never be in a hurry to buy a car? The same goes for selling one, too. Never be in a hurry to sell a car. You will never get full market value for it. Sure, all of us would like to sell our cars within a few days, but sometimes it takes longer to find the right buyer. If you are anxious to sell, you certainly don't want to show it when a potential buyer is looking at your car. If they sense you are in dire need of money, they will low-ball you with an offer. So make like the poker player with a full house and be deadpan.

As for advertising, you can start by putting a "For Sale" sign in the window. Make sure you don't put it where it will cause a dangerous blind spot. The rear driver's-side passenger window would be a good place.

If you live in a local area where people post ads on bulletin boards around post offices, grocery, and hardware stores then take advantage and make up some posters. As long as it's free, why not? A nice color photo of your car attached to your ad will make it stand out from the rest.

For paid advertising, I always start in the local newspaper classifieds and suggest you do the same. Your local paper is probably the most popular publication in town and anyone who's looking for a car will certainly be scanning the ads for one. A weeklong ad should be a good start.

In all advertising, the more lines you need the more you will be charged. Keeping it short and sweet will save you some money. The goal is to make it reach your target buyer(s) and be appealing at the same time.

You should start by including the year, make, and model. Include engine type i.e., 350, V6, 4-cyl, etc., only if your model offered more than one engine size. Mention whether it has an automatic transmission or 4-speed, 5-speed, etc. If your car offered either 2- or 4-door models, mention what yours is. If your car has low mileage then you definitely want to include it. If it has high miles, don't mention it. State any other key features that it may offer like convertible, four-wheel-drive, etc. Also, if your car has air-conditioning and you live in the south where air is highly desirable, mention it as well. Some people, myself included, can't live without AC.

If you are the original owner or the second owner, mention it. If you had some major work, like a rebuilt engine for which you have receipts, mention that too. You only have so much room in the ad and you can't include everything, so all that middle-of-the-road stuff you had done to your car can be described later over the phone. An ad stating new brakes or a new battery or a new clutch really won't sell your car any faster.

The ad's whole purpose is to attract the right person, and finding the right person will be easier when you list the key features of your car. For example, if you fail to mention that your car is a 5-speed, everyone interested in an automatic model will be calling to find out what yours is, wasting their time as well as yours.

As for all those frilly things like power windows, power this and that, and your fancy stereo, you can save it for your pitch over the phone or, if your car has them all, use one word - *loaded*.

Finally, one last descriptive word for the hook. You want to end your ad with something like *Dependable, Clean,* or *Garaged*. So a properly worded ad might go something like these:

'79 Chevy Camaro. Rebuilt 350
w/receipts, auto, loaded, runs xlnt,
2nd owner, clean. $2400 555-1234

'84 Toyota Corolla. 4 dr, 5 spd, air,
95k. Dependable $2700 555-4321

Always abbreviate where you can. If you're not sure what to shorten, the ad consultant in the classified department who does this all day long can help you. Make sure you include your asking price; otherwise you will be plagued by callers wanting to know your price. Remember, dealers read the ads daily, always looking for a deal. Listing the price will screen them out along with the wishful thinkers.

THE PHONE CALLS

You need to prepare yourself for the kind of questions people will ask. If you were selling the '79 Camaro above, the first question I would ask, after confirming the information in print, is who rebuilt the engine? So have your receipts out and ready. I would also want to know how many miles are on the car and how many miles are on the rebuilt engine. If you are the second owner and all this work was done before you bought it, study that receipt. All this information should be on there.

Other questions I would ask are, "How long have you owned it? Who was the original owner? How often was the oil changed and who did the maintenance? Has it ever been in an accident" or "Are there any dents or scratches? Are all the power options working? Is anything broken or in need of repair?" If you've owned the car for some time, you should know all this off the top of your head. If you don't, find out. Know your car.

Always let callers ask the first round of questions. When they seem finished, offer the information about the middle-of-the road stuff like your new tires, new brakes, new battery, etc. If they seem interested and they haven't already asked, don't forget to mention the window dressings like all your power options and that fancy stereo.

In used car selling there are times to fib and times to be honest. Many people will probably ask you how long you've had it for sale and if anyone else has looked at it yet. No matter how long you've had it for sale or how many people have looked at it, the answer to these two questions is always the same. You have just put it up for sale and no one has seen it yet.

This makes people hungry to come over for a look. Deals don't last and if you tell them that three others have looked at it and it didn't sell, it tells the buyer that either there's something wrong with your car or you have it priced too high. But when no one else has looked at it, interest is stirred with thoughts of a deal ripe for the picking.

On the other hand, if your car has a major problem, such as rust or damage from an accident, don't lie and try luring people over without mentioning it over the phone. It's not like they won't notice. Be honest and up front with them; otherwise you will be causing hard feelings, wasting people's time and yours. There's nothing worse than driving a long way to look at a car that you never would have bothered with had you been properly informed in the first place.

THE APPOINTMENT

When you're selling a car, try to be accommodating and flexible when making the appointment. Everyone works, so weekends are most likely when you'll get people over. However, if someone wants to come over early on a weekday morning or on a weeknight, take the time to do it.

This is a sign of someone who needs a car right away, who will probably give you close to your asking price, if not all, providing he likes your car. If you push him off until the weekend he may find something else by then and you'll never hear from him again. So it may be well worth it to show up late for work or miss your game down at the ball field.

Before you give up time at work, it is wise to find out ahead that the caller is indeed a serious buyer and not just a browser. You will find that many people will call, act interested, tell you they're coming, and then never show. They either found another car and didn't have the decency to call and cancel or, for reasons that are beyond me, are afraid to say they are not interested and tell you they're coming anyway when they have no intention of doing so. This can be extremely frustrating when you are taking time out of your busy schedule to accommodate them.

The way to weed these people out is easy. Just ask them directly, "Are you really coming over? I don't want to take time off work for nothing." When they say yes, ask them to call back right before they are ready to come by and you will give them directions then. If you hear back from them, you can count on them coming by. If you don't hear from them, they would have been a no-show.

If someone calls and wants to come over now, ask for his phone number just in case something comes up and you need to reschedule. About fifteen minutes before he is supposed to arrive, call the number. If you get no answer or a recording with his name on it, then it looks like you have a serious buyer on his way over. If you get a wrong number, go to your ball game.

When the person shows up to look at your car, be friendly and greet him by his name (which you found out over the phone), shake his hand, and make eye contact. I know this sounds like something a used car salesman would do, but what the heck, at this point you *are* a used car salesman. Hang back and let the buyer look it over. Some people, you will find, are timid about looking at a car, so don't force information upon them. Make them feel comfortable. If they want to know something, they will ask.

While they are looking, you have a folder with all the related receipts and the title of ownership at your disposal. The current registration should already be in the car. Offer to show these if they would like. Also offer to open the hood and trunk. Timid lookers may be too shy to ask and because you spent so much time **cleaning**, you want to show off all the car's selling points.

When they want to take it for a test drive, go with them even if they have a passenger and you must sit in your cramped back seat. I'm always leery about letting strangers take off in my car. It's not that I'm so worried about them stealing it. I worry more about them getting into an accident. People not familiar with your neighborhood might run a stop sign, get lost, or mixed up. If you're there in the car you can direct them where to go. Have a route all picked out in advance. Just like I discussed in the **Test Drive** chapter, you want to direct them to a quiet street and to a freeway or the equivalent.

When you go with them on the test drive, there's nothing wrong with talking about the weather in a friendly way, but don't sit there talking nonstop about irrelevant topics. This is very annoying and the buyers may think you are trying to distract them from a hidden problem. Just sit back and leave the floor open. Let them ask the questions. If they bring up unrelated topics, then it's okay to partake.

After the test drive, the buyers may want to check under the hood again to look for oil leaks, etc. If anything is in question, offer to let them have their mechanic look it over--at their expense, of course. Sometimes people gain your trust and won't find it necessary. So all that is left to do is agree on a price. If they do prefer to have their mechanic look at it, try to be as flexible as possible.

NEGOTIATING

When it comes time to negotiate, the advice is pretty much the same as I outlined in the **Negotiation** chapter, except now the roles are reversed. The seller, whether he takes your car to a mechanic or not, will try to find things wrong with it to use as bargaining leverage to get you to lower your price. Fortunately, you have already padded your asking price in anticipation of this and are ready to come down some.

In settling on a price, there are some things to consider. Even though you have determined in your mind what your bottom price is, if you and the buyer have come to within $100 or $200 of meeting each other and he doesn't want to budge, you have to ask yourself these questions. Is my selling price realistic? Has my phone been ringing? Are there others interested in looking at it, or is this person the only one so far? Is there anything wrong with this car which the buyer is unaware of that makes it not worth as much?

If you haven't been getting much of a response from your ad, you may want to succumb to the buyer's offer. However, if your phone has been ringing off the hook, then hang tough and only give in a little. When you inform the buyer that you have had lots of calls, this will make him realize that if he wants your car, then he better act quickly with a sweeter offer.

Let's say you are selling your well-maintained car for $2,500. Except for being used, there really is nothing wrong with it. What do you do if someone comes over and low balls you with a $1,500 offer? Chances are the person is a dealer and trying to tempt you with cash. He will simply take the car and sell it off his lot, making at least $1,000 if not $1,500. So if this happens, hang tough and don't let him intimidate you. Just smile and say "Sorry." He might ask you what your bottom price is. If he does, tell him and stick to it no matter what.

Another tip in negotiating is don't advertise your bottom price followed by the word *firm*. Someone like me is going to offer a lower price anyway and, chances are, if your phone hasn't been ringing, you'll give in.

Always pad your price. There's something about negotiating that gives people a sense of accomplishment when you lower your price to meet them. In their eyes they just saved some money and this makes them feel good. When you advertise a *firm* price with the intention of not budging, people tend to make lower offers regardless. When you don't budge, they sometimes become too proud to give in to your full price. So you are forced to make a choice: you either go below your bottom price or lose the sale.

Also, don't let yourself get suckered by someone who wants your car, but won't have the money until either he sells his car or money comes in from some other unpredictable source. THE FIRST PERSON WHO COMES UP WITH THE CASH GETS YOUR CAR. If he wants to leave a deposit and have you hold the car until he gets his finances together, fine. Ask for a $100 non-refundable deposit and hold the car for no more than a week. You want to be sure he is serious about buying your car.

If by the end of the week he comes up empty, but still wants you to hold your car for him, get another $100 deposit. Should he default, you pocket the deposit for the inconvenience. In the meantime, write down all the numbers to callers who called on your ad so if the deal falls through, you can call them back.

When you go to transfer your vehicle, have all the paperwork in order. If you have lost your title, get a duplicate made up BEFORE you are ready to sell. In California it takes four to six weeks to get a duplicate title sent to you. It makes it easier to sell your vehicle when you have all the documents.

Even though it can be easily done, people are not always comfortable transferring a vehicle into their name without a title. Sometimes they will refuse until you have the title in your hands, so not having the title can sometimes cost you a sale. You can't blame them though. You may be on the up and up, but they don't know you from Adam. Without the title, they might think the car is stolen or has a lien against it. So have all your paperwork in order: title, registration, state inspections and, for us Californians, odometer disclosure and smog certificates.

A FEW LAST TIPS

•When a person buys a used car without a warranty, he is buying the car "as is". This means if he is driving it home on the day of the sale and the transmission blows up, he can't take it back to the seller for repair or his money back.

For your own protection, I recommend you write this out on the handwritten receipt. John Doe has purchased such-and-such vehicle "as is" on such-and-such day for such-and-such amount. Cars bought and sold between private parties are always assumed "as is", but writing it out on the receipt protects you in case someone comes back claiming you somehow misled them.

•If you're a single woman selling your car, it's not advisable to be alone when showing your car to strangers, especially while on the test drive. Arrange to have a friend with you. It's a sad society we live in today. You just can't trust people anymore.

•Never sell your car by setting up a payment plan where someone takes your car and pays you in monthly installments. YOU ARE NOT A BANK. Even if it's a trusted friend or relative, don't take the chance. Accidents do happen and cars do get stolen, and if he failed to get insurance you're out of a car. If he suddenly becomes unemployed and can't make the payments, you get to choose between being patient until he gets a new job, taking the loss, or becoming the ugly repossessor. Of course, by this time you and you're "trusted" friend or relative will no longer be speaking.

•In setting a price on your car, don't let the Blue Book sway you too much. It's just a price guide. The real world goes by supply and demand. But it is good to know the book price to use as a reference during negotiations. The best way to see what the market is on your car is by studying the classifieds for a month or so. To take this one step further, you could call the ads for cars identical to yours a week or two after they were published to find out if they sold and for how much.

THE NINE GOLDEN RULES TO SELLING YOUR CAR

1) Detail your car before selling it
2) Have all necessary titles, inspections, and paperwork in order
3) Know your car's market value
4) Publish effective ads
5) Separate the looky loos from the serious buyers over the phone
6) Be flexible when making the appointment
7) Negotiate, but don't give away your car just to get rid of it
8) No financing anyone, even friends or relatives.
9) Never be in a hurry to sell a used car

PART III:

CARING FOR YOUR USED CAR

CHAPTER 7:

CAR CARE

Now that you have gone through all the trouble of finding a good used car, and paid a mechanic to check it over, TAKE CARE OF IT! Between the previous owner and the maintenance schedule in your owner's manual, find out immediately if the car needs service now and/or what it will be needing next. Anything that's due, get it taken care of pronto. The baby is now in your hands.

By taking care of your car, you're protecting your investment. Remember, the better shape it's in when it's your turn to sell, not only will you get top dollar for it, but it will be easier to sell as well. The following chapter offers car maintenance information, gasoline concerns, warm-up procedures, and some great car care tips which will enable you to enjoy many problem-free miles.

YOUR OWNER'S MANUAL

You most definitely want the owner's manual to your car. So if it has been lost, check with the dealer about getting a replacement for your model and year. If they're no longer available, try to get a manual for your model from a later year. If you strike out there, then you'll be forced to buy a repair manual for your car, which can be found at most auto parts stores.

If you like to tinker, obtaining a repair manual wouldn't be such a bad idea anyway. The repair manual offers much more insight on your car's maintenance and repairs for the do-it-yourselfer, with how-to chapters on everything from changing a fuse to a complete engine overhaul. The troubleshooting section alone is worth the price.

Do understand, though, that a repair manual would be a *supplement* to your owner's manual, not a substitute. Owner's manuals offer much more detailed information about your car, such as cold morning starts, when to shift the manual transmission, dash features, etc. So don't get a repair manual as a substitute when an owner's manual is available. However, when they're not available, a repair manual is better than no manual.

The maintenance schedules in both manuals will offer important information you need to know about when to adjust/replace the valves, idle speed, transmission fluid, air filter, spark plugs, timing, timing belt, etc. It all goes by mileage or time, whichever comes first.

Most owner's manuals offer two or more maintenance schedules to follow, depending on how you drive your car. There may be a "normal" driving maintenance schedule, a "unique" driving maintenance schedule, a "severe" driving maintenance schedule, and/or a "severe weather" driving maintenance schedule. The confusing thing about all this is what's considered normal driving in most owner's manuals isn't really normal at all.

How many of us never do any stop-and-go city driving or repeated short trips or experience dusty, rough or salt-laden roads or prolonged periods of freezing cold, heat, humidity or rain? That pretty much sums up all the climates in the United States, doesn't it?

Most owner's manuals consider "normal" driving to be without any of these elements, but is that possible? Don't let this fool you. You would have to live in a dry (but not dusty) climate that never gets hot or cold, where the roads are smooth and your driving is from point A to B with no stops in between, with trips being a minimum of 5 miles long, giving the engine sufficient warm up.

This certainly would be ideal for your car, but it's an unlikely reality. So forget the "normal" maintenance schedule in your owner's manual and go with the "severe" or "unique" schedule. You want the one that calls for more frequent servicing, which will help you keep your car in tip-top shape.

ABOUT OIL

I had mentioned earlier about the importance of regular oil changes. Let me stress this again. OIL SERVICE IS THE MOST IMPORTANT THING YOU CAN DO FOR YOUR CAR. When you read your owner's manual and it recommends oil changes every 5,000 miles, 7,500 miles, or even 10,000 miles, this is one section of your owner's manual I want you to ignore. Whether you change your own oil or you have it done at a lube center, CHANGE YOUR OIL AT LEAST EVERY 3,000 MILES OR 3 MONTHS, WHICHEVER COMES FIRST - NO IFS, ANDS, OR BUTS! Every 2,000 or 2,500 miles would be even better.

There have been many studies on the frequency of oil changes and its effect on engine parts. One thing always holds true: the more frequent the oil changes, the longer the engine will last. It doesn't matter if you own a Volkswagen or a Mercedes, you will get more miles and value out your car with frequent oil changes than someone who doesn't.

For example, a car that has had its oil changed every 3,000 miles may get more than 200,000 miles on the engine before there's a need for major repairs, whereas the same car that had its oil changed every 7,500 miles may not even make it to 100,000 miles before it needs engine work. God forbid if you change your oil every 10,000 miles!

Consider the facts. Oil is still cheap. If you change your oil every 3,000 miles, then in 200,000 miles you would have changed your oil 66 times. Let's say your car takes five quarts of oil. Multiply this times 66 equals 330 quarts. This, multiplied by $1.50 per quart equals $495. Now, using the same formula to figure how much you would spend on oil at intervals of 7,500 miles, I came up with $195--$300 dollars less. It doesn't make sense to save $300 in oil so you can run your $1,500 engine out of life twice as fast.

Clearly, frequent oil changes are the way to go. Even if your car has 90,000 miles on it and the previous owner changed the oil every 7,500 miles, don't think it's too late to do any good by increasing the oil changes now. It will. You truly slow down the engine's aging process with more frequent oil changes.

For those few of us who drive little, like less than 1,000 miles a month, make sure you change your oil every three months regardless. Even though you may have put as little as 1,500 miles on your car in this time span, the oil in your engine still breaks down with age and needs replacing. So low-mileage people, change oil by time intervals, not mileage, and you will be doing your car a big favor.

Now what grade of oil should you use? That information is in your owner's manual, or you can call your local dealership and ask them to look it up for you. Most likely it will be a 10W-30 or a 10W-40. Depends on where you live. As for what brand to use; everyone has their favorites. If you stick with a recognized name brand, you'll be fine. I don't recommend off-brands that you've never heard of. They may be okay and they may not. Why take a chance? OIL IS THE LIFE-BLOOD OF YOUR CAR!

And one last note about oil filters. CHANGE THE OIL FILTER EVERY TIME YOU CHANGE THE OIL. I've noticed some owner's manuals recommend that you change the filter every *other* time you change the oil. If this is what yours says, then ignore that part of your maintenance schedule as well. Again, oil filters are cheap. Why pour in five quarts of fresh oil only to have half a quart of filthy oil in the used filter that will pollute your new oil immediately? This doesn't make sense. Do your engine a big favor, change the filter every time and keep it clean in there.

If you were lucky and bought your car from someone who kept a maintenance record of all service and repairs, then you know exactly where you are with your car and when it's due for the next oil change. If the seller didn't keep records and doesn't know, or claims it was changed recently, but the oil looks dirty, get it changed pronto (honey-colored oil is fresh, while dark brown or black oil is old and due for a change).

OIL BURNERS

Most cars with more than a 100,000 miles on them will use oil. As a matter of fact, you can come to expect it from any car with an odometer reading in the six-figure range. This is not something to freak out about. As your engine wears, some oil will slip by the rings and burn off relatively clean. I'm not talking about cars billowing blue smoke behind them. That's another story. Cars that have high miles will usually use half to one-and-a-half quarts between a 3,000-mile oil change without any notice of smoke out your exhaust pipe. When you get up to two quarts, you'll be paying your mechanic's rent soon.

The key advice for proud owners in the six-figure odometer club is, not surprisingly, KEEP A CLOSE WATCH ON YOUR OIL LEVEL! Try not to let it get more than half a quart low. When you first get your car you should be checking the dipstick weekly. After a few months of close observation, you can gauge just how fast it's using oil either by mileage or time intervals. Use this for future reference to know when it's time to check/add the next half quart. The proper oil level will keep your motor purring like a content kitty for many more miles to come.

OTHER FLUID CONCERNS

If you bought a car with an automatic transmission from someone who didn't keep a maintenance record, ask when was the last time the transmission was serviced. If the previous owner doesn't know, get it done pronto. Ditto goes for manual transmission cars with upward of 100,000 miles on them. If the owner doesn't know when or if the gear oil has ever been changed, do it now. It's not that expensive. If your car has a differential (rear wheel drive), have this oil changed at the same time. After all, they work together and this is a good way to start out with a clean slate.

It's worth noting here that most manual transmissions require a heavy 90-weight gear oil, but not all do. Some of today's front-wheel-drive transaxles require a much thinner 30-weight oil. If-90 weight is mistakenly used, gears can burn up by not receiving the proper lubrication, resulting in costly repairs. As you can imagine, a simple mix-up like this could easily happen at a quick lube center where some inexperienced or uninformed attendant is changing your oil. MAKE SURE YOU KNOW WHAT WEIGHT OIL GOES IN YOUR TRANSMISSION, AND RELAY THAT INFORMATION TO THE ATTENDANT WHO CHANGES IT!

As for the rest of the car's maintenance, you will have to work from the evidence you have. Aside from the oil and transmission fluid, make sure you check all the other fluids: brake, power steering (if your car has it), hydraulic clutch (if your car has it), battery water level (if it's not maintenance free), windshield washer fluid, and the coolant level.

When the engine is cold, look inside your radiator to see what color the fluid is. It should be a greenish yellow color. If yours is anything but that, have your cooling system flushed and new coolant added. If it is yellowish green, you will be okay for now. Make a note to check it during your next oil change. Most cars today offer a reservoir tank for the coolant with a high and low mark in which to keep the fluid between. You can find the tank by locating the small hose that comes from under the radiator cap and following it to the unit.

Periodically check the coolant level and make sure you keep it between those marks. Follow directions according to your owner's manual and mix the correct ratio of coolant and water. Always use distilled water for your cooling system and for batteries that are not maintenance free. Water from your tap may have high concentrations of minerals which could corrode the inside of your radiator or harm the cells in your battery.

LUBE CENTERS

Quick lube service stations make life easy for car owners who don't have the time or know-how for car maintenance. For about 20 bucks you're in and out in 10 minutes with a fresh oil change. You don't even get out of your car! When you first buy your car, I recommend paying extra for the deluxe service where they do a fourteen-point check service. Not only do they change your oil, they also check fourteen points on your car, topping off all fluids. Some will even vacuum and wash your windows!

When it's all said and done, the attendant will inform you of any fluids that were low, anything that may be leaking, if your coolant needs a flush, if an air cleaner is in need of replacement, or any other service that may need immediate attention or be just around the corner. For those who don't know much about cars, quick lube service centers are a time and money saver. And remember to save your receipts! Check the yellow pages under service stations for quick lube centers in your area.

TIRES

Get into the habit of periodically checking your tires' air pressure. Too much or too little air can cause your tires to wear prematurely. You can pick up a pressure gauge at any auto parts store for a couple of bucks and keep it in your glove box where it's handy. Air pressure should be checked when the tires are cold or you may get a biased reading. A short trip to your local service station won't matter, but a half-hour trip on a hot day could.

When you are checking air pressure, also check the tires' tread for uneven wear. If you have been good about keeping the right amount of air pressure and start to notice uneven wear, it usually means you have developed an alignment problem. Let it go, and you will also be paying for new front tires along with your front-end alignment. Early detection will allow you to save your existing tires and some cash.

Also, a good way to squeeze a few extra thousand more miles out of your tires is by having them rotated regularly. Most tire centers will rotate your tires for free, provided the tires are the brand they sell. Even if you didn't purchase the tires yourself, contact the tire store that sells the brand tires that are on your car and ask to have them rotated. Most tire shops won't require a receipt. Get your tires rotated every 10,000 miles.

ENGINE PING AND GASOLINE

If you notice your engine has started knocking it could be a couple of things. Your engine may be a few degrees out of time, indicating the need for a tune-up. Or, if it is a manual transmission, you may be driving in the wrong gear and lugging the engine, which is a no-no (manual transmission people, make sure you are in the right gear). However, if you're not due for a tune-up, the most likely reason for engine knock is poor-quality gas from your last fill-up. Engine run-on, where your car wants to keep running after it is turned off, is also a symptom.

Not all gasolines are created equal. An 87 octane rating at one station may not be the same as the 87 rating at another, and the same goes for the higher octane ratings as well. It gets involved, but the octane rating posted at the pumps is reached by adding together the ratio of the Research Octane Number and the Motor Octane Number and then dividing it in two. Because these ratios can vary without affecting the posted octane rating, the gas at one station may be much better quality than the gas at another.

Good advice here would be to avoid the el cheapo gas stations and stick with the nationally known chains. You will pay a few cents more at the pump, but you get more than that back through better mileage and an engine that will run smoother and last longer.

So before you pay to have your car tuned up because it's been pinging, suspect poor quality gas and do some experimenting. Start by trying the 87 octane rating at several reputable stations. If this doesn't clear up the knocking, bump up to the 89 octane rating and start over. Sooner or later you will fill up with a tank of gas that has cleared up your engine ping and Eureka! You have found your gas station. Stick with them. And it would be safe to assume that if the

89 octane rated gas at station X down the street that cleared up the knocking, then the 89 octane gas at station X across town or across the country, for that matter, will have the same effect.

Just as gasoline is different, so are cars. Some cars are more sensitive to the quality of gas, while others run fine and dandy on the cheapest gas in town. Usually this becomes evident when you have made a change in vehicle ownership. As described above, do some experimenting.

For fuel-injected cars, a quality grade of gas is imperative. Engines with fuel injectors usually require a higher rated octane than carbureted ones. Check your owner's manual for recommendations or call your car's respective dealer and ask the service department what they suggest.

TUNE-UP

As your owner's manual will show, regular tune-ups are a good form of preventive maintenance. Periodically, all cars need them to continue running their best. Because the change in your engine is very gradual and most owner's manuals call for a tune-up before the engine has had a chance to sound bad, the need for a tune-up is usually not noticeable. This is the time to forget the "if it ain't broke don't fix it" rule. Get your car tuned when it's due.

A minor tune-up, or minor service as it's now called, is usually every 30,000 miles. It would include the following: new oil and oil filter, air cleaner, spark plugs, fuel filter, coolant flush, chassis lubrication, valve adjustment, and idle speed adjustment for carbureted engines. Inspection of drive belts, fuel lines, steering linkage, brake system, exhaust system, cooling system, and all fluid levels should be performed as well. Some cars will also have their manual/automatic transmission fluids changed at this time, while others may be on their own schedule. This should clear up any hard starting or rough idle problems.

A major tune-up, or major service, which is usually every 60,000 miles, would include all of the above with the addition of a new timing belt (if your car has one), fuel filter, EGR valve, PVC valve; replacement of worn belts and hoses may be necessary as well. Keep in mind that all cars' tune-up intervals vary. Go by what your owner's manual says.

REPAIR FRAUD

The best way to avoid automotive repair fraud is to always insist on a written estimate (in many states, this is the law). Request that any changes in the estimate can only be made with your approval, and ask that the old parts be saved for your inspection.

If you ever pay for automotive work that wasn't done correctly, or feel you have been sold unnecessary parts or service, California has the Bureau of Automotive Repairs to help address these problems. They require you to file a complaint form along with copies of your receipts for the work done. You will then be assigned a representative who will mediate between you and the repair shop for either new work or a refund, depending on the situation.

The Bureau also offers *A Consumer's Guide to Automotive Repair,* which is a free brochure that tells you how to select a good mechanic, outlines your rights as a consumer, and shows you how to file a complaint. You can obtain a complaint form or the brochure by calling 800-952-5210. If you don't live in California, start by contacting your state's Consumer Protection Agency. If they can't help, they should know who can.

ENGINE WARM-UP

There has been much confusion lately about the proper way to warm up your car. Actually it boils down to two conflicting opinions--the old rule of thumb and the new rule of thumb.

The old rule of thumb was to warm up your car before driving it, especially in the morning. The colder the temperature outside, the longer you would need to warm it up. In the summer 60 seconds may be sufficient, while in the frigid winter it may take 4 or 5 minutes. Also, when first driving off, you should take it easy on the gas pedal until the car reaches normal operating temperature.

The theory behind the old rule of thumb is that when your car sits, all the oil ends up in the pan. When you start your engine in the morning, it takes a minute or two for the oil to warm up and circulate throughout. Starting your cold engine and driving off without first warming it up would put extra wear on moving parts before the oil has sufficiently coated the insides. With the first minute or so of metal against metal, day after day after day, people who didn't warm up their cars supposedly found themselves paying for repairs much sooner than the those who religiously did their warm-ups. Makes sense, right? Fasten your seat belts.

The new rule of thumb is to let your engine warm up only 10 to 20 seconds and drive off slowly, taking it easy on the accelerator until the engine is up to normal operating temperature. In frigid temperatures, a few more seconds of idling may be necessary before driving off.

The theory behind the new rule of thumb is that because most engine wear occurs when the engine is cold, the sooner you warm up to normal operating temperature, the sooner there won't be cold engine wear. An engine warms quicker when it is being driven rather than when it's sitting there idling for a minute or two.

Both opinions agree that most engine wear occurs between the time it is first started and the time it reaches normal operating temperature. This usually requires 5 to 10 miles of driving, depending on the outside temperature and how long ago the engine was last run.

Both opinions also agree that driving during the warm-up process should be taken slow and easy until the engine has reached normal operating temperature. Slow and easy means being very gentle on the accelerator to gradually increase your speed and to barely go the speed limit. No hard accelerations or revving the engine when it's cold.

So which warm-up method should you practice? It appears that the old rule of thumb may apply to older engines, while the new rule of thumb may apply to today's sophisticated motors. To be certain which category your car falls under, check your owner's manual and follow what it says about warming up the car, or call your car's respective dealership and ask the service department their opinion. Whichever warm-up method you use, the most important step is driving slow and easy until the car has reached normal operating temperature.

CAR CARE TIPS

•Whenever you drive your car it's a good idea to take it easy all the time, not just during the warm-up process. When people take it easy on their cars, their cars return the favor and take it easy on their pocketbook. When you constantly accelerate hard and brake hard, you shorten the life of all related parts--namely the engine, transmission, clutch, and brakes. Get the picture? So get into the habit of taking it easy. Your car will love you for it.

CAR CARE   111

•Previous owners who kept records and all their receipts make life easy for those of us who buy their cars. Regardless of what your previous owner did, this is what you need to do. Every time you change the oil, write down the mileage and the date and the grade of oil and type of filter you use. Every time you buy tires, replace the brakes, change the spark plugs, etc., log it down and keep those receipts!

If you have a computer you can open a new file and keep everything organized. If you don't, keep a file in your desk drawer for all those receipts and start a ledger for the oil changes. It will be easier to sell your car when a potential buyer has proof that the car has been well cared for. The next owner will appreciate it.

•If you're like me and like to tinker under the hood, but hate to get grease under your fingernails, go to your local drug store and by a box of surgical gloves. They are thin and tough and when you are through with surgery just peel them off and you still have clean fingernails and are now ready for your hot date.

•You may think I'm crazy with this one, but the best way I have found to keep battery terminals from corroding is by coating them with imitation maple syrup right before you go for a drive. The heat will cause the syrup to crystalize into a hard glass. If you need to give someone a jump-start you can easily break it off with the jumper cables. Recoat at your earliest convenience.

•The best way to detect leaks is by putting a flat piece of cardboard under your car. The next day you can pinpoint where the leak is coming from by the location of drops and the type of fluid found on the cardboard.

•As a safety measure, most cars with a manual transmission won't start unless you push in the clutch pedal first. That way, if the car is in gear and you try to start it, there's no danger of it lunging forward. If your car doesn't have this feature, get in the habit of doing it anyway. Not only is it a safe practice, it also saves on your battery and starter motor.

•If you do most of your own auto maintenance, watch for sales on oil, filters, etc., from your local auto parts store and stock up when the opportunity arises. Then when your car is due for an oil change, there's no running around trying to find the best price on oil and filters, etc.

- Contrary to the common method of warming up your engine before an oil change, I do just the opposite. Warming up the engine puts a fresh coating of oil on all the internal parts of your engine as well as some in your oil filter. However, a cold engine has all the oil in the pan and the oil filter is mostly drained. Because the cold oil is already in the pan, it really doesn't take any longer to drain out and you won't get messy oil dripping out of the oil filter when you change it.

- When searching for a place to park in a parking lot, get in the habit of picking a spot away from the crowd. This will greatly reduce the risk of someone tagging your car door. Besides, unless you are an aerobics trainer or professional sports star, we all could use a little more exercise in our lives.

- Along with parking away from the crowd is searching for a shady parking spot. This will save your dash, upholstery, and keep your paint from fading as well as keeping the inside of your car from becoming an oven. Also, leaving your windows cracked a half-inch will help alleviate the baking effect.

- Manual transmission people, when parking your car, get in the habit of setting your emergency brake before putting it in gear. This leaves the tension off your gear box and on your brakes where it belongs.

- Make sure all your dash gauges and lights are working properly and you understand what they mean. Temperature gauge, oil pressure gauge, battery gauge--if one of these light up while you're driving, you better know what to do or you may burn up your engine. You can find this information in your owner's manual or call your car's respective dealership and ask the service department to explain them.

- Once you have owned your car for a while you will become familiar with its sound. Always listen for any changes to that sound. Your car may send some early signals of repairs that are just around the corner. Even if it requires going to your mechanic, follow up on any unfamiliar noises and find out what's causing them, pronto. Early detection of a necessary repair can save dollars by getting it taken care of before other related parts become damaged.

CAR CARE   113

•Do-it-yourselfers who change your own oil, make sure you discard your old oil properly. No pouring it back into the ground where it came from or throwing it in the trash where it will end up in the ground somewhere else. Used motor oil is highly toxic to our ground water. Save the used motor oil in jugs and periodically dispose of it at a recycling center that accepts it. Check with your city's public works department or with the service stations in your area. Some service stations accept used motor oil.

•Standard drivers, proper downshifting can make your car's brakes last many thousands of miles longer while the extra wear to your clutch is practically non-existent. Look in your owner's manual for proper downshifting methods for your car and get into the habit.

•If you live in a rainy climate you may need to have your chassis lubed more often than stated in your owner's manual. Constant splashing of water on the underside of your car can wash away grease and replace it with dirt. Suspension and steering linkage is expensive to replace.

•Get in the habit of gauging your gas mileage and know your average miles per gallon. Should that average begin to drop, it's a sign for a tune-up...or you may have caught some other minor repair before it becomes an expensive one.

•With many bumpers painted or plastic these days, you can't remove an unwanted bumper sticker using a razor blade without scratching it up good. Try using a hair blow dryer or squirt on some WD-40 and let it soak. Either of these will usually do the trick. WD-40 is also great for unwanted window decals.

•California residents, save all your old emission test reports. With results every two years revealing how many parts-per-million of hydrcarbons your car is emitting, this is valid evidence of how well you kept your car in tune, which is nice to show to potential buyers in the future.

•When in need of interior parts or body parts, consider the salvage yard. Things like a new bumper, tail-light lens, door panel, or front seat can be very expensive when bought new through a dealer. But at the salvage yard, you can get them for a fraction of the cost and they may be just as good as new. Make the auto graveyard your first call.

• If you notice bird poop on your car or someone eggs you on Halloween, get it washed off as soon as possible. Bird poop and eggs have acid in them that will eat away at your paint and permanently scar it.

THE SEVEN GOLDEN RULES OF CAR CARE

1) Read and understand your owner's manual completely
2) Have your oil changed at least every 3,000 miles or three months, whichever comes first
3) Have your car tuned up as required
4) Become accustomed to your car's sound and listen for changes in that sound.
5) Be aware of repair fraud
6) No hard driving on cold engines
7) Always keep records of all service and repairs performed on your car

APPENDICES

Appendix A:

The Used Car Buyer's Manual Directory of Reliable Used Cars

Italics denotes **Best Used Car Bets**

Acura Integra '86-'95
Acura Legend '86-'95
BMW 3-Series '85-'95
BMW 5-Series '85-'95
BMW 7-Series '85-'95
Buick Century '86-'95
Buick Electra V6 '85-'90
Buick Le Sabre (3.8 L) '85-'95
Buick Park Avenue V6 '91-'95
Buick Regal '84-'95
Cadillac De Ville '80-'95
Cadillac Eldorado '80-'95
Cadillac Fleetwood '80-'95
Cadillac Seville '80-'95
Chevrolet Camaro '80-'95
Chevrolet Caprice '80-'95
Chevrolet Cavalier '84-'95
Chevrolet Celebrity V6 '82-'91
Chevrolet Corvette '80-'95
Chevrolet Lumina '90-'95
Chevrolet Nova '85-'88
Chrysler Le Baron GTS '85-'88
Chrysler New Yorker (4cyl) '83-'88
Dodge Aries '84-'89
Dodge Caravan '84-'95
Dodge Challenger '80-'83
Dodge Colt '80-'94
Dodge Omni '80-'90
Dodge Ram 50 Trucks '83-'93
Dodge Spirit (except turbo) '89-'94
Ford Crown Victoria '82-'95
Ford Explorer '91-'95
Ford Festiva '88-'93
Ford Mustang V6 '83-'86
Ford Probe '89-'95
Ford Taurus V6 '88-'95
Ford Thunderbird (except 4cyl) '83-'95
Geo Metro '89-'95
Geo Prizm '89-'95
Geo Storm '90-'93
Geo Tracker '89-'95
Honda Accord '80-'95
Honda Civic '80-'95
Honda Prelude '80-'95
Infiniti G20 '91-'95
Infiniti J30 '93-'95
Infiniti M30 '90-'92
Infiniti Q45 '90-'95
Isuzu Trooper '91-'95
Isuzu Trucks '84-'94
Lexus ES250 '90-'91
Lexus ES300 '92-'95
Lexus LS400 '90-'95
Lexus SC300 '92-'95
Lexus SC400 '92-'95
Lincoln Continental '80-'95
Lincoln Mark VI '80-'83
Lincoln Mark VII '84-'92
Lincoln Mark VIII '93-'95
Lincoln Town Car '81-'95
Mazda 323 '86-'94
Mazda 626 '80-'95
Mazda 929 '88-'95

APPENDICES 117

Mazda GLC '80-'85
Mazda Miata '90-'95
Mazda MVP '89-'95
Mazda MX-6 '88-'95
Mazda Protege '90-'95
Mazda RX-7 '80-'95
Mazda Trucks '80-'95
Mercedes-Benz 190E '84-'93
Mercedes-Benz 280E, CE/SE '78-'81
Mercedes-Benz 380SE, SL '81-'85
Mercedes-Benz 450SL '78-'80
Mercury Capri '80-'86 & '91-'94
Mercury Cougar (except 4cyl turbo XR-7) '84-'95
Mercury Grand Marquis '83-'94
Mercury Sable '88-'95
Mercury Tracer '88-'95
Mitsubishi Diamante '92-95
Mitsubishi Eclipse '90-'95
Mitsubishi Galant '85-'95
Mitsubishi Mirage '85-'95
Mitsubishi Montero V6 '89-'95
Mitsubishi Trucks '83-'95
Nissan Altima '93-'95
Nissan (Datsun) Trucks '80-'95
Nissan 200SX '80-'88
Nissan 240SX '89-'95
Nissan 300ZX '84-'95
Nissan Maxima '81-'95
Nissan Pathfinder '87-'95
Nissan Pulsar NX '83-'90
Nissan Sentra '82-'95
Nissan Stanza '82-'92
Oldsmobile Ciera '82-'95
Oldsmobile Cutlass & Cutlass Supreme '80-'95
Oldsmobile Delta 88 & Eighty Eight '80-'95
Oldsmobile Ninety Eight '80-'95
Plymouth Acclaim '89-'95
Plymouth Colt '83-'94

Plymouth Horizon '80-'90
Plymouth Laser '90-'94
Plymouth Reliant '86-'89
Plymouth Sundance '87-'94
Plymouth Voyager '84-'95
Pontiac 6000 '86-'92
Pontiac Bonneville '80-'95
Pontiac Firebird '80-'95
Pontiac Sunbird '86-'93
Saab 900 '80-'95
Saab 9000 Turbo '86-'95
Saturn SL, SC, & SW '91-'95
Subaru Justy '87-'94
Subaru Legacy '90-'95
Subaru Loyale '90-'94
Subaru Sedan '80-'89
Subaru SVX '92-'95
Subaru XT '85-'91
Toyota 4Runner '84-'95
Toyota Camry '83-'95
Toyota Celica '80-'95
Toyota Corolla '80-'95
Toyota Cressida '80-'92
Toyota Land Cruiser '80-'95
Toyota MR2 '85-'89
Toyota Previa '91-'95
Toyota Supra '86-'95
Toyota Tercel '84-'95
Toyota Trucks '80-'95
Toyota Van '84-'89
Volkswagen Cabriolet '85-'93
Volkswagen Golf '85-'95
Volkswagen Jetta '81-'95
Volvo 240 '87-'93
Volvo 740 '85-'92
Volvo 760 '83-'90
Volvo 940 '91-'95

Appendix B:
Inspection Checklist

Part One: Visual Inspection

	OK?	Cost to Repair/Replace - Notes
1) Body Damage - Accident		
Check for over spray		
Check for mismatched paint		
Eyeball body and seams		
2) Body Damage - Rust		
Check wheel wells/fenders		
Check flooring		
Check trunk		
Tap and listen to areas in question		
Rust repair? Method used		
3) Tires and Suspension		
All tires match?		
Tread depth?		
Test shock absorbers		
Does car sit level on flat surface?		

4) Fluids
Check oil - clean? dirty? full? low?
Check under oil filler cap
Auto transmission fluid - color? smell?
Coolant - color? reservoir level?
Inspect radiator/AC fins for damage

5) Air Filter - Clean? Dirty?

6) Check All Hoses

7) Check Drive Belts

8) Fluid Leaks
Oil seepage - oil pan? valve cover?
Check underside for: Oil?
Transmission fluid?
Coolant?
Brake fluid?

9) California Emissions
Check sticker - underside of hood
Check gas filler tube

10) Check Tailpipe
Color? light gray/brown is normal

	OK?	Cost to Repair/Replace - Notes
11) Glass		
Cracks or chips?		
12) Sunroof		
Factory or custom?		
Check full range of movement		
13) Interior - Check:		
Front seats		
Rear seats		
Head liner		
Carpeting		
Dash		
Odometer reading		
Glove box		
Windows - crank-up/electric		
Locks - power/manual - use key		
Heater		
Air conditioning		
Emergency brakes		
Horn		
Head lights - low/high beams		
Dome lights		

APPENDICES 121

Dash lights
Windshield washer/wipers
Stereo
Convertible tops - open & close
Tilt steering
Other power options
14) Luggage Compartment
Opens with ignition key and remote?
Spare tire?
Jack?
Lug wrench?

Part Two: The Test Drive

1) Listen to Engine	OK?	Cost to Repair/Replace - Notes
Cold idle		
Odd sounds? - valves?		
Lifters?		
Exhaust leak?		
Undetermined		

2) Check brakes
Solid pedal?
Brakes evenly? - pulls to one side?
Brake noises - squeaks? grinds?

3) Check Alignment
Car drives straight or wanders
Steering wheel shimmy?

4) Check Transmission
Check reverse - noises?
Manual - shifts through gears easily?
Stick shift pops out of any gear?
Automatic shifts smoothly?

5) The Open Road
Car's performance at 50 mph
Check alignment again
When finished, check again for leaks

6) Check Receipts
Receipts for - repairs? new parts?
Maintenance records?
Odometer in accordance with receipts?

7) Seller's Character
Car's appearance?
Home and yard appearance?

8) At Your Mechanic
Highlight all items above in question

9) Check Recall Information
Recall Hotline #1-800-424-9393 or call the respective dealership with the VIN

Additional Notes

Closing Note

The publisher wishes to invite your criticisms about this book. Feel free to inform us of any mistakes, oversights, unclear subject matter, or any important points that we had missed. Your suggestions will be considered for future editions. Also, we would enjoy hearing your success stories that resulted from this manual. To reach us, write to the following address:

Pyramid West Publishing
P.O. Box 830
Newbury Park, CA 91319

-Order Form-

Use this form to order additional copies of *The Used Car Buyer's Manual* and *The Used Car Buyer's Manual II*.

Title	Quantity	Price	Total
UCBM		$9.95	
UCBM II		$7.95	
	CA residents please add 7.25% sales tax.	+	
	Shipping & Handling	+	
		Total	$

Discounts: Order three or more books and take 10% off the price.

Shipping & handling: Add $2.50 for the first book and .75¢ for each additional book. Send check or Money Order to:

**Pyramid West Publishing
P.O. box 830
Newbury Park, CA 91319**